Accounting for Non-Accountants

KEY TO AN UNDERSTANDING OF ACCOUNTING

BY

John N. Myer

CO-ORDINATOR OF THE ACCOUNTING PROGRAM

THE MANAGEMENT INSTITUTE

DIVISION OF GENERAL EDUCATION AND EXTENSION SERVICES

NEW YORK UNIVERSITY

AMERICAN EDUCATION COUNCIL

LARCHMONT, NEW YORK

by arrangement with

NEW YORK UNIVERSITY PRESS

First Printing, March, 1957
Second Printing, May, 1958
Third Printing, September, 1958
Fourth Printing, November, 1958

Library of Congress Catalogue Card No. 56-5431

PRINTED IN THE UNITED STATES OF AMERICA

Foreword

THE COMPLEXITIES of modern business make it almost necessary for all persons managing a business to have some knowledge of accounting. To be sure, they normally delegate accounting matters to a professional accountant. But in order to be able to understand the results of the accounting processes as found in the financial statements compiled by the accountant, it is essential to know the significance of the terms employed and the procedures used in arriving at conclusions. This knowledge is not easily acquired unless a person has been properly instructed, since the accountants use an empirical technique leading to results that usually can be interpreted only by those who have been introduced into the mysteries of the profession. This knowledge Professor Myer is here attempting to supply.

The reader may be surprised at Professor Myer's contention that accounting is not a science and that its conclusions are not precise. In fact, he seeks to show (particularly in Part V, on *Understanding the Accounting Data*) that the *modus operandi* of accounting is akin to that of the arts rather than to that of the sciences. He further attempts to demonstrate that while the technique of debit and credit employed by the accountant is precise, the conclusions it leads to are not precise since accounting deals with matters that cannot be measured precisely, not only because of the nature of the things to be measured but also because of a faulty unit of measurement, the dollar. It is for this reason, Professor Myer states, that the accountants have adopted conventional rules implemented by a series of postulates and applied on the basis of personal judgment.

A knowledge of accounting is important not only to business executives but also to those engaged in other professions in which accounting data are used. This is evidenced by the popularity of Professor Myer's course in the Management Institute where the present volume has been developed.

PAUL A. McGHEE, *Dean*
Division of General Education and
Extension Services
New York University

February, 1957

v

Preface

ANYONE WHO commences the study of accounting is, of course, a non-accountant. The term is used in the title of this book in the sense of one who neither is nor intends to become a professional accountant. In this category are such professional men and women as engineers, lawyers, economists, statisticians, credit men, investors, and business executives, all of whom from time to time require a knowledge of accounting in connection with their professional work. For these and for persons preparing themselves for such professions, this book has been prepared. A book of problems to accompany it is available for schools and for those who desire to study privately.

Since it is assumed that the reader is not preparing himself for the profession of accountancy but rather to gain a knowledge of how accounting is done and the significance of its results, the financial statements, the emphasis is on *understanding* rather than *doing*. The four chapters in Part V have been written with this in mind.

The scope of the book is that of the usual one-year elementary college course. Its brevity has been achieved by a simple approach and a direct sequence which avoids the introduction of procedures that must later be discarded. Another aid toward brevity is that alternative methods of performing various phases of accounting have been omitted since they are of no particular interest to the non-accountant and would tend to confuse him. The method selected in each case is the one the author considers is most generally used.

The approach employed is through a discussion of accounts. This is most natural since accounting technique is basically a matter of debiting and crediting accounts in accordance with the accepted principles of accounting and at periodic intervals summarizing their contents. The account has thus been made the central feature of accounting. The books of original entry are a means of collecting data to be put into the accounts; and the balance sheet is a summary of the position of the accounts after the books have been closed as of a certain date.

The author wishes to express his gratitude to those who have helped in the production of this work: to Milton R. Stern, of the staff of the Division of General Education and Extension Services of New York University, for suggesting the name for the course given by the author in the Management Institute that has been used as the title for this book; to Robert C. Trethaway, Managing Editor of the *Journal of Business Education,* for permission to use certain material. previously contributed to that magazine; to Grace LeRoy for designing the book; to Hugh G. Duncan of the Vari-Typer Corporation for various helpful suggestions; and to Denis Sinclair Philipps, Director of the Management Institute, for constant encouragement.

JOHN N. MYER

February, 1957

Contents

I.

RECORDING AND CLASSIFYING FINANCIAL TRANSACTIONS

1. Assets and Their Sources

ACCOUNTING is the art of keeping the financial records of a business. The financial records are those that are stated in terms of money.

Records of business transactions exist from even the earliest known civilizations, although the early records are crude and lack systematic arrangement. Modern financial record-keeping had its beginnings in Italy some six centuries ago, when such cities as Venice and Genoa had become great commercial centers. The growth of commerce naturally was accompanied by a need for business records, so in response to this need, a system of record-keeping was created. Because the records were kept in books the system was given the name of *bookkeeping*.

You might now want to ask, "What is the difference between 'bookkeeping' and 'accounting'?" The answer would be that there is no difference. But if a distinction is to be made it should be said that bookkeeping is the routine record-keeping part of accounting. Today much of this routine is done on machines.

In addition to the routine making of records, accounting is concerned with the use of the records. From them are prepared various summaries or statements. Through interpretation of these statements information is obtained which is of great importance to those who are responsible for the management of a business and to others interested in its affairs, such as bankers and other credit grantors, stockholders, prospective investors, and governmental agencies.

Accountancy is the profession that devotes itself not only to practicing the technique of accounting but also to devising special systems for the various types of business, verifying the records that have been compiled by others, and presenting facts about a business. One who is a member of the profession of accountancy is known as an *accountant*.

3

ASSETS

The things possessed by a business are called *assets*. But in order to be an asset within the scope of accounting a thing must have the quality of being measurable in terms of money. For example, although a supply of fresh air in an office is very important to those who work there, the accountant does not regard fresh air as an asset. It is what the economist calls a "free good." You cannot say that it is worth a specific number of dollars. It might be said that to the accountant "if it cannot be measured in terms of money, it is not an asset."

The assets of a business comprise not only cash and such property as land, buildings, machinery, furniture and fixtures, merchandise, and so forth, but also claims for sums of money against individuals or other enterprises.

CAPITAL

Where do the assets come from? They are put into the business either by the owner or owners or they are put in by others.

The total of that portion of the assets put in by the owners, stated in terms of money, is referred to as their investment or *capital*. This word has thus been given a meaning in accounting different from that in economics, where it is used to denote the property or wealth possessed by a business enterprise.

LIABILITIES

When persons who are not the owners put assets into a business, such persons are known as creditors. Contribution by creditors takes place when the asset cash is loaned to the business or when merchandise or other assets are sold to it but payment therefor is to be made at some future time. Creditors who have sold property to the business expect to receive from it a specific sum of cash at a certain date, in accordance with the terms of sale.

From the time money is loaned or goods are sold to a business until the date of payment the creditors are contributors to the assets possessed by the enterprise. Creditors, therefore, have an interest in the business and may be considered temporary investors.

The amounts of money owed to the creditors by a business are known as its *liabilities* because it is liable to the creditors for the sums owed, that is, it must pay them such sums.

SOURCES OF
ASSETS

Since there are two sources from which assets are derived—creditors and owners—it follows that at any particular time the total of the assets will be equal to the total of the contributions of the cred-

4

itors and owners. The contributions of the creditors and owners are referred to as their interests or equities in the assets.

The fact that the assets of a business must be equal to the equities of the creditors (liabilities) plus those of the owners (capital) may be expressed in the form of the equation:

THE BASIC AXIOM

$$\text{ASSETS} \ = \ \text{LIABILITIES} \ + \ \text{CAPITAL}$$

This is a self-evident truth or axiom that requires no proof. However, the following is offered:

The assets of a certain business are stated at $10,000. If $8,000 of these were put in by the owners and $2,000 by the creditors, then, substituting the dollar amounts in the above equation, we have:

$$\$10,000 \ = \ \$2,000 \ + \ \$8,000$$

The axiom, that the total of the assets (measured in terms of money) is equal to the liabilities plus the capital of a business is the basis of the technique of accounting.

Assets come into a business not only by direct contribution by the owners and creditors but also as a result of the operation of the business. For example, if the owner performed a service for a client for which he was paid in cash, the assets would be increased by the amount of this cash. Such increase in assets through earnings is known as *income* to the business. In more formal language it is called *revenue*.

EFFECT OF OPERATIONS: INCOME

The increase in assets through the operation of the business by the owner is in the nature of a contribution by him and so increases his interest, the capital. Thus, capital may be increased not only by direct contribution by the owner but through the earning of income.

A business may earn income in various ways. The greater part of the income is usually from its regular activity. If it is a trading business, the income will be derived mainly from the sale of merchandise. If it is a business that renders service, such as a garage, a laundry, or a trucking business, the income will be largely the result of the charges for the service. But in addition there may be income in the form of commissions, interest on promissory notes of customers, rent of premises let to others, and similar sources.

5

EXPENSES

In contrast with the increase in capital through the earning of income, there is usually also a decrease in capital as a result of *expenses* incurred in order to earn income. The salaries paid to employees, the rent paid to the landlord, the interest on indebtedness, and the cost of telephone and other services are examples of such expenses.

There are thus two forces constantly at work that affect the capital: income, which increases it, and expenses, which decrease it.

When expenses are not paid for at the time they are incurred but are to be paid for at some future time, the amount of such expenses is recorded as a liability. Thus liabilities may increase not only as the result of contributions by creditors but also through the incurring of expenses by the business.

NET INCOME OR
NET LOSS

When the total of the income, or revenue, of a business for a certain period of time, such as a year, exceeds the total of its expenses for that period, the result is *net income* for the period. Net income causes an increase of the capital.

When the total of the expenses for the period exceeds the total of the income, the result is a *net loss* for the period. A net loss results in a decrease of the capital.

THE CASH AND
ACCRUAL
BASES

There are two bases on which accounting may be practiced; they are the *cash basis* and the *accrual basis*.

On the cash basis income is considered as earned only when payment is actually received; and expenses are taken into consideration only when actually paid for.

On the accrual basis income is considered earned when goods have been sold or services have been performed, although payment may not have been received. In similar manner, expenses are taken into consideration as soon as they have been incurred, although they may not have been paid for.

The use of the cash basis is more or less limited to small businesses that have hardly any accounting records other than a cash register to keep a record of receipts and a bank checkbook on the stubs of which a record of payments is kept.

This book is devoted to an exposition of accounting procedure on the accrual basis.

6

2. Debit and Credit

YOU WILL NO doubt agree that a business should have a record of its property, or assets. Those interested in the business require such information as the amount of cash available, the sums of money the customers owe to the business, the extent of its stock of merchandise (if it is a trading business), and the equipment owned to carry on its activities, such as a building, office and salesroom furniture, automobiles, and so forth.

A record of the liabilities of the business is also necessary because they represent sums of money that have to be paid to the creditors at certain dates in the future. In addition, information with respect to the capital is required because the owners are naturally interested in knowing the extent of their equity in the business.

Then, too, there is need for a record of the various kinds of income and expense in order that the net income (or net loss) may be measured for managerial and tax purposes.

ACCOUNTS

The above-mentioned records are kept in a book called the *ledger*. This book consists of many units known as *accounts*.

The ledger contains: a record of, or account with, each kind of asset, showing the amount of such asset in terms of money; an account with each of the creditors, indicating the liability or sum of money owing; an account showing the capital of the owner or owners; and an account with each kind of income and each kind of expense.

The following form is generally used:

Debit Side   *Credit Side*

7

Note that the account is divided vertically into two identical parts. The left side is called the *debit side* and the right side the *credit side*.

As used in modern accounting, the terms *debit* and *credit* distinguish the two sides of an account and have no other significance. They apply to all kinds of accounts. On one side are recorded the increases in the item for which the account is constructed and on the other side the decreases in that item. The side on which increases or decreases are recorded depends on the kind of account, as will now be shown.

RECORDING TRANSACTIONS: (1) ASSET ACQUIRED BY CONTRIBUTION OF OWNER

The receipt of or increase in an asset is recorded on the debit side of the appropriate asset account.

Let us suppose that on March 1, 1956, Robert Harrison invests $1,000.00 in a business. Since the business receives cash, an asset, this fact is recorded on the debit side of the Cash account in the following manner:

Cash

1956						
Mar.	1		1,000.00			

When an asset comes into a business a record is made not only of this fact but also of the source of the asset. This is done on the credit side of the account with the source. If the source is the owner, the record is made on the credit side of the owner's Capital account.

Thus, since Robert Harrison, the owner, puts the $1,000.00 into the business, the record of this fact is made in the account Robert Harrison, Capital, as follows:

Robert Harrison, Capital

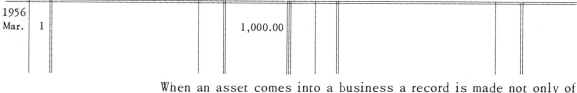

			1956					1,000.00
			Mar.	1				

When an amount has been recorded on the debit side of an account, that amount is referred to as *a debit* and it is said that the account has been *debited* with that amount. Similarly, when an amount has been recorded on the credit side of an account, that amount is re-

8

ferred to as *a credit* and it is said that the account has been *credited* with that amount.

Considering the transaction just used as an example, it is said that the increase in cash is recorded as a debit and the increase in capital as a credit or that the account Cash is debited and that the account Robert Harrison, Capital is credited.

You have now seen that an asset account increases on the debit side and that the Capital account increases on the credit side. Also that there are two contrasting records: the asset (a debit) and the source of the asset (a credit).

Let us now assume that on March 5, 1956, Robert Harrison purchases furniture from William Smith for $500.00 on 10 days' credit; that is, Smith contributes $500.00 worth of furniture to Harrison's business with the expectancy of receiving $500.00 in cash on March 15 from Harrison. **(2) ASSET ACQUIRED BY CONTRIBUTION OF CREDITOR**

In this transaction furniture comes into the business; and since the receipt of an asset is recorded by a debit in the account with that asset, the account Furniture is debited:

Furniture

1956							500.00							
Mar.	5													

It has been shown that when an asset is contributed to the business the account with the source of the asset is credited. So in this case the account with William Smith is credited:

William Smith

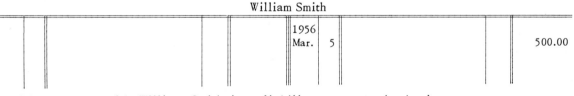

The account with William Smith is a liability account: the business owes $500.00 to Mr. Smith for the furniture purchased from him and is to pay him this sum on March 15.

You have already seen that asset accounts increase on the debit side. Now you see that liability accounts, like the Capital account, increase on the credit side.

9

**(3) ASSET AC-
QUIRED IN
EXCHANGE FOR
OTHER ASSET**

An asset may be acquired by surrendering another asset, usually cash.

Suppose that on March 7 Harrison purchases $100.00 worth of furniture for cash.

Since an increase in an asset is recorded as a debit in the account with that asset, it follows that a decrease in an asset is recorded as a credit in the asset account. Accordingly, when the acquisition of furniture is recorded as a debit in the Furniture account, the Cash account is credited. These accounts in the ledger of Robert Harrison now appear thus:

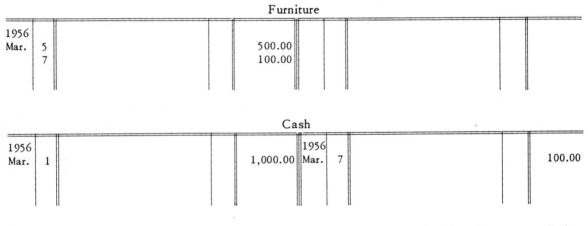

Furniture

| 1956 Mar. | 5 | | 500.00 | | | | | | |
| | 7 | | 100.00 | | | | | | |

Cash

| 1956 Mar. | 1 | | 1,000.00 | 1956 Mar. | 7 | | | | 100.00 |

**(4) LIABILITY
LIQUIDATED BY
SURRENDERING
AN ASSET**

Liabilities are most commonly paid, or liquidated, by surrendering cash.

Let us now suppose that on March 15 Harrison pays Smith the $500.00 he owes him.

Since an increase in a liability is recorded as a credit in the account with the creditor, it follows that a decrease in a liability is recorded as a debit in the liability account. Therefore, the payment of cash to liquidate the liability to Smith is recorded as a debit in the account with William Smith and a credit to Cash. These accounts now appear as follows:

William Smith

| 1956 Mar. | 15 | | 500.00 | 1956 Mar. | 5 | | | | 500.00 |

10

Cash

| 1956 | | | | | 1,000.00 | 1956 | 7 | | | 100.00 |
| Mar. | 1 | | | | | Mar. | 15 | | | 500.00 |

Sometimes a liability is liquidated by creating a different kind of liability.

Let us now assume that instead of paying cash to William Smith on March 15 Harrison finds it inconvenient to pay Smith the $500.00 and that Smith is willing to accept a 30-day promissory note in lieu of cash, but bearing interest at the rate of 6 per cent per annum to compensate him for waiting for the money. This transaction decreases the liability in the form of the account payable to William Smith and increases a new form of liability, that of a note payable. It is recorded by a debit to William Smith and a credit to Notes Payable. The accounts affected appear thus:

(5) LIABILITY LIQUIDATED BY CREATING ANOTHER LIABILITY

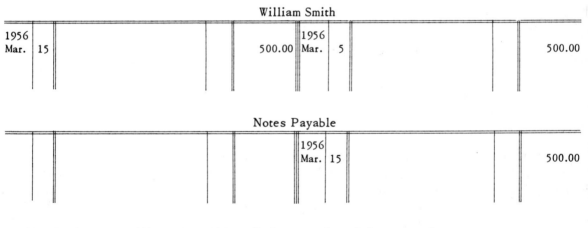

William Smith

| 1956 | | | | | 500.00 | 1956 | 5 | | | 500.00 |
| Mar. | 15 | | | | | Mar. | | | | |

Notes Payable

| | | | | | | 1956 | 15 | | | 500.00 |
| | | | | | | Mar. | | | | |

As the interest will not be paid until the maturity of the note, the entry for this interest is not made at the time the note is given but at the time the note and the interest are paid.

You have seen that transactions which increase the capital appear as credits in the Capital account. Therefore, since the earning of income increases the capital, each income transaction might be re-

(6) INCOME AND (7) EXPENSES

11

corded as a credit in the Capital account. Similarly, since expense transactions decrease the capital, they might be recorded as debits in the Capital account.

However, in order that there may be a classified record of the amount of each kind of income and each kind of expense, there is opened in the ledger a separate account for each type of income and each type of expense, instead of recording the income and expense items in the Capital account. These income and expense accounts are in the nature of subdivisions of the Capital account and record the increases and decreases in the capital caused by the earning of income and the incurring of expenses.

There will thus be separate accounts for such forms of income as income from fees, income from investments, income from commissions, interest income, and so forth. In similar manner, there will be separate accounts for the various expenses: rent, salaries, office supplies, telephone, interest, and so forth.

If services are performed by the business for James Dale and he pays a fee of $135.25 in cash for such services, this income transaction is recorded in the following manner:

> *Debit* Cash, $135.25
> *Credit* Income from Fees, $135.25

If office supplies priced at $15.85 are purchased from the Adams Stationery Company and paid for in cash, the record for this expense transaction is:

> *Debit* Office Supplies, $15.85
> *Credit* Cash, $15.85

OFFICE SUP-
PLIES: ASSET
OR EXPENSE?

You might say that at the time the office supplies are purchased an asset comes into the business in the form of tangible property. That is true. But since this type of asset is used up rapidly and thus its cost becomes an expense in a short period of time, it is usual to regard the cost of such items as an expense immediately. This avoids the more laborious process of first recording the receipt of an asset and then shortly thereafter recording the conversion of that asset into an expense.

ENTRIES ON THE
ACCRUAL BASIS

If in the case of the services rendered to James Dale, as mentioned above, it were agreed that the client should pay at a future date, an account would be opened with him to record his indebtedness

12

to the business and this account, representing a claim against the client, is an asset account. The transaction would be recorded in the following manner:

Debit James Dale, $135.25
Credit Income from Fees, $135.25

When payment is received from Dale the entry is:

Debit Cash, $135.25
Credit James Dale, $135.25

It is important for you to understand that whether the services are rendered for cash or on credit the income account Income from Fees, which records the increase in capital caused by the transaction, is credited; and that in either instance an asset account is debited, either Cash or an account with the client that records his indebtedness to the business. Such an account with a client or customer is called an *account receivable* since it records an amount to be received from him.

If the purchase of office supplies from the Adams Stationery Company mentioned above were made on credit instead of for cash, the transaction would be recorded as follows:

Debit Office Supplies, $15.85
Credit Adams Stationery Company, $15.85

Upon making payment the entry is:

Debit Adams Stationery Company, $15.85
Credit Cash, $15.85

Note that whether the office supplies are purchased for cash or on credit the expense account Office Supplies, which records the decrease in the capital caused by the transaction, is debited. When the office supplies are purchased for cash the asset account Cash is credited and when purchased on credit the account with the creditor, in this case the Adams Stationery Company, which records the liability to that creditor, is credited. Such an account with a creditor is called an *account payable* since it records the amount to be paid to him.

From the foregoing you have seen that the accounts which record the sums owing to the business from customers, or clients, as the case may be, are called accounts receivable; and that the accounts which record the sums owing by the business to creditors are called accounts payable. These titles, accounts receivable and accounts

ACCOUNTS AND NOTES RECEIVABLE AND PAYABLE

payable, refer to two groups of accounts: those with customers and those with creditors, respectively. It is obviously necessary to have a separate account with each customer and each creditor, in order to be able to determine at any time how much each customer owes to the business and how much the business owes to each creditor.

Sometimes a customer pays an amount owing by giving a promise to pay, or promissory note, in payment. The receipt of such note is recorded by a debit to the account Notes Receivable and a credit to the customer's account (an account receivable). If a note for $150.00 is received from William Hill in payment of that amount owing in his account, the entry is:

> *Debit* Notes Receivable, $150.00
> *Credit* William Hill, $150.00

Similarly, as has already been shown, when the business gives a promissory note to a creditor, the amount of this note is debited to the account with the creditor (an account payable) and credited to the account Notes Payable. If such note for $200.00 is given by the business to Frank Good in payment of that amount owing in his account, the entry is:

> *Debit* Frank Good, $200.00
> *Credit* Notes Payable, $200.00

Your attention is directed to the fact that a separate account is kept for each account receivable and each account payable but that only a single account is used to record all the notes receivable and a single account to record all the notes payable. The reason for this will be found in a later chapter.

(8) OWNER'S WITHDRAWALS

When the owner of a business makes a withdrawal of funds such withdrawal reduces the amount of his capital. However, as in the case of the income and expense accounts, the withdrawals are not recorded in the Capital account but are debited to a separate Drawing account in order that there may be a statistical record of such withdrawals.

When, for example, Robert Harrison withdraws $75.00 from his business for personal use, the entry is:

> *Debit* Robert Harrison, Drawing, $75.00
> *Credit* Cash, $75.00

SIMPLE AND COMPOUND ENTRIES

In each of the illustrations above there is one debit and one credit. But sometimes a transaction is of such a nature that more than one

14

debit or credit is required. For example, if when office supplies are purchased from the Adams Stationery Company on credit a chair priced at $20.00 is also purchased, the entry would be:

> *Debit* Office Supplies, $15.85
> *Debit* Furniture, $20.00
> *Credit* Adams Stationery Company, $35.85

Also, assuming that the note receivable from James Dale for $150.00 is a 60-day note bearing interest at the rate of 6 per cent per annum, then at maturity Mr. Dale pays the amount of the note, $150.00, plus $1.50 interest, or a total of $151.50. The entry for the payment then is:

> *Debit* Cash, $151.50
> *Credit* Notes Receivable, $150.00
> *Credit* Interest Income, $1.50

When an entry consists of one debit and one credit it is referred to as a *simple entry;* when there are more debits or credits than one, the entry is called a *compound entry.*

The accounting record of every transaction discussed above consists of one or more debits and one or more credits, and the sum of the debits is equal to the sum of the credits. From this it follows that for a series of transactions the sum of all the debits would be equal to the sum of all the credits; and, further, that the sum of all the debits in the ledger of a business would be equal to the sum of all the credits in that ledger. **EQUALITY OF DEBITS AND CREDITS**

In making or discussing the record of a transaction, it is customary to place the debit first, followed by the credit.

The abbreviation used by accountants for the word "debit" is *Dr.* and for "credit" the abbreviation is *Cr.*

Because of the fact that in the procedure here explained there is both a debit and a credit for each transaction, or what might be regarded in the nature of two entries, the term *double entry bookkeeping* or *double entry accounting* has been given to such procedure. **DOUBLE ENTRY BOOKKEEPING**

The types of transactions that commonly occur in business have been discussed above. They are summarized as follows: **SUMMARY OF DEBIT AND CREDIT**

1) Asset acquired by contribution of owner,
   Debit: Account with asset acquired.
   Credit: Capital account.

15

2) Asset acquired by contribution of creditor,

Debit: Account with asset acquired.
Credit: Account with creditor (a liability account).

3) Asset acquired in exchange for other asset,

Debit: Account with asset acquired.
Credit: Account with asset surrendered.

4) Liability liquidated by surrendering an asset,

Debit: Account with liability liquidated.
Credit: Account with asset surrendered.

5) Liability liquidated by creating another liability,

Debit: Account with liability liquidated.
Credit: Account with liability created.

6) Earning of income
   a) By receipt of cash,

Debit: Cash.
Credit: Account with type of income earned.

   b) By creation of a claim against a customer or client,

Debit: Account receivable with customer or client (an asset account).
Credit: Account with type of income earned.

7) Incurring of expense
   a) By payment of cash,

Debit: Account with kind of expense incurred.
Credit: Cash.

   b) By creation of a liability,

Debit: Account with kind of expense incurred.
Credit: Account payable with creditor (a liability account).

8) Asset withdrawn by owner,

Debit: Drawing account.
Credit: Account with asset withdrawn (usually cash).

The effects of changes in the assets, the liabilities, and the capital are thus recorded in the respective accounts in the following manner:

Assets	*Debit or Credit*
Increase	Debit
Decrease	Credit
Liabilities	
Increase	Credit
Decrease	Debit
Capital	
Increase	Credit
Decrease	Debit

Subdivisions of Capital	Debit or Credit
Income	
Increase	Credit
Decrease	Debit
Expenses	
Increase	Debit
Decrease	Credit
Drawing Account	
Increase	Debit
Decrease	Credit

The difference between the greater and the lesser side of an ac- **BALANCE OF**
count is called the *balance* of the account. Thus in Robert Harrison's **AN ACCOUNT**
Cash account, shown on page 11 and reproduced below, the total of
the debit side is $1,000.00 and the total of the credit side is $600.00.
The balance of the account is $400.00, signifying that the amount of
the asset cash that Robert Harrison owns at this time is $400.00.

Cash

1956					1956				
Mar.	1	400.00		1,000.00	Mar.	7			100.00
						15			500.00
									600.00

The accountant from time to time totals both sides of the accounts
and inserts the totals in small, light pencil figures. This procedure is
known as *pencil footing* the accounts. He then inserts the balance on
the greater side as in the illustration.

Since the balance of an account represents the excess of increases
over decreases, the balance of an asset account will be on the debit
side. It is, therefore, called a *debit balance*. The balance of a liability account and of the Capital account will be a *credit balance,* because these accounts increase on the credit side. For the same reason
the owner's Drawing account will have a debit balance, the income
accounts credit balances, and the expense accounts debit balances.

If both sides of an account are equal there exists no balance and
the account is said to be *in balance*. Thus, the account payable to
William Smith, page 11, is in balance as of March 15, 1956.

3. Accounts in the Ledger

CLASSIFICATION
OF ASSETS AND
LIABILITIES

SOME ASSETS are of a relatively permanent nature; it is necessary for the business to have them in order to carry on its activities. Examples of such assets are: a building, furniture and fixtures, and automobiles. These assets the accountant classifies as *fixed assets*.

In contrast to these, there are other assets which are continually moving into and out of the business, or are being converted from one form to another. Examples of such assets are: cash, notes receivable, accounts receivable, and the merchandise inventory (in the case of a trading business). These assets the accountant classifies as *current assets*.

The accountant also classifies the liabilities into two general groups. The grouping is made with regard to the time when the liability must be paid. If the liability is to be paid within a year, it is classified as a *current liability;* if due within more than one year, it is placed in the category of a *long-term liability*. Of course, as the maturity of a long-term liability approaches to within a year, it becomes a current liability.

Examples of current liabilities are: notes payable and accounts payable (if due within a year, which is usually the case). An example of a long-term debt is a mortgage on a building maturing in more than one year.

CHART OF
ACCOUNTS

The accountant often compiles a chart or list of the accounts that he has opened in the ledger. A chart of the accounts in the ledger of Henry Johnson, compiled shortly after he had started a new business, is shown on page 19.

The groups of accounts are usually arranged in the ledger in the order shown in the chart of accounts on page 19: current assets, fixed assets, current liabilities, long-term liabilities, the Capital account, the owner's Drawing account, the income accounts, and the expense accounts.

There is no prescribed order for the arrangement of the accounts within the fixed asset and long-term liability groups. The accountant

18

HENRY JOHNSON
CHART OF ACCOUNTS

Assets

CURRENT ASSETS:
Cash
Notes receivable
Accounts receivable
William Adams
Goldsmith and Marshall
John Wood
FIXED ASSETS:
Building
Office furniture
Automobiles

Liabilities

CURRENT LIABILITIES:
Notes payable
Accounts payable
Hubbell and Blair
Stellar Corporation
LONG-TERM LIABILITIES:
Mortgage payable (on building)

Capital

Henry Johnson, Capital
Henry Johnson, Drawing
INCOME:
Income from fees
EXPENSES:
Rent
Office supplies
Postage
Salaries
Miscellaneous expense

uses his discretion in arranging these accounts. But there is a definite order in which the accounts are customarily placed in the current asset and current liability groups.

The current asset accounts are placed in the order: Cash, Notes Receivable, the various accounts receivable, Merchandise Inventory (in the case of a trading business).

The arrangement from cash to merchandise is in the order of liquidity. Cash is the most liquid of all assets, for it is readily available to be converted into other forms of assets or to be used to liqui-

19

date liabilities. The notes and accounts receivable come next in order of liquidity since they will in due course be converted into cash. Next comes the merchandise (in a trading business) which must be sold, converted into receivables, and then into cash. (In a cash sale the merchandise, of course, is converted directly into cash.) The arrangement mentioned is in accordance with what is known as the "trading cycle" of a business, for the movement of assets, as a trading business conducts its operations, is from merchandise into receivables, and then into cash.

The order in which the current liability accounts are placed in the ledger is that of urgency. The most urgent obligations are the notes payable because they must be paid precisely on the day on which they mature; therefore, the account Notes Payable is placed first in the current liabilities group. This is followed by the various accounts payable.

ACCOUNTING
FOR THE
CAPITAL

The three important forms of business ownership organization are:

Individual proprietorship
Partnership
Corporation

The individual proprietorship form is that in which the business is owned by one person. In the partnership form the business is owned by more than one person, but usually a rather small number. No governmental sanction is required to organize a business in the form of an individual proprietorship or partnership. The corporation is a form of business ownership organization that is organized under governmental supervision, that of the state.

The accounting for the income, expenses, assets, and liabilities of a business is identical in all three forms of organization. However, there is a difference in accounting for the capital.

As you have seen from Chapter 2, in the ledger of an individual proprietorship the capital or investment of the proprietor or owner is shown in a Capital account. Any withdrawals made by him are debited to a Drawing account.

In accounting for a partnership there is a separate Capital account for each of the partners, in order to keep a record of the investment or interest in the business of each of them. It follows, of course, that there is a Drawing account for each of the partners.

The capital of a corporation is divided into *shares* of *capital stock*. Those who own the shares are the owners of the business and

20

are known as *stockholders*. The name given to the account that records the capital is Capital Stock.

You have seen from Chapter 2 that when the accountant uses the word *capital* it signifies the excess of the assets over the liabilities. But the economist uses this word in a different sense. To him, *capital* refers to materials produced by a business or used to produce income.

ACCOUNTING CAPITAL AND ECONOMIC CAPITAL

Economists speak of capital as "wealth possessed by a business" and this may be in the form of "production goods" such as machinery and other equipment or "consumption goods," the merchandise in process of manufacture or ready for sale.

There thus exists a seeming conflict between the accountants and the economists because the word *capital* has been clothed with different technical meanings in economics and in accounting to meet the needs of each of these fields. Such technical uses of words are common in all the various fields of human activity.

21

4. Books of Original Entry

IT HAS BEEN shown in Chapter 2 how business transactions are recorded in the ledger. Each transaction, according to the technique of accounting, consists of one or more debits and one or more credits. Similar debits and credits are gathered together and classified in accounts.

For example, all the debits representing the acquisition of, or increase in, furniture are posted to the debit side of an account with Furniture. The total of these debits indicates the amount, in terms of money, of all the furniture acquired by the business. The corresponding credits usually affect the account Cash or various accounts payable, and such credits are recorded in the appropriate accounts.

There is, however, need for a record that will show each transaction in its entirety. When it is desired to obtain information from the accounting records with respect to the acquisition of furniture, it may not be sufficient to learn that the furniture has been increased. It may also be necessary to know how the furniture was acquired: whether by the payment of cash, by the creation of a liability, or in some other way. It is thus desirable to have in one place a record showing both the debit and the credit parts of each transaction.

Because of the need for a record of each transaction as a whole, before the transactions are recorded in the ledger they are entered in chronological sequence in other books and from these *books of original entry* the data are transcribed into the ledger. The ledger is thus a secondary record.

The process of carrying the data from the books of original entry to the ledger is known as *posting*.

As a result of this twofold record of business transactions, the books of account show each transaction both in its entirety and also analyzed into its debit and credit components to show its effect on the assets, the liabilities, or the capital, or some combination of these three groups of accounts.

A special book of original entry is used for each type of transaction that occurs with considerable frequency and all other transactions

22

are entered in what is known as the *journal*, called by some the *general journal*. Since the number of types of transactions that occur frequently varies with the kind of business and its size, the number of books of original entry used by one enterprise will vary from those used by another.

There is shown below the form commonly used for a journal. THE JOURNAL

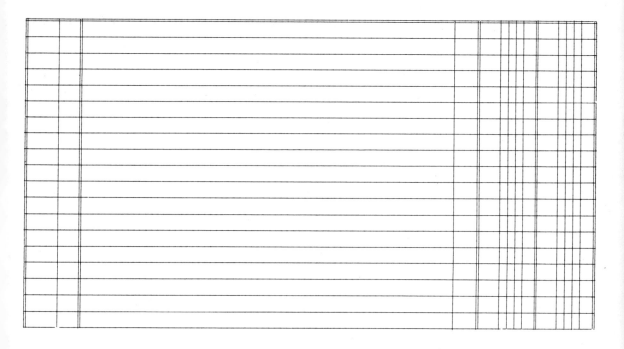

In accounting for a very small business it is conceivably possible to use only one book of original entry, the journal. In fact, this is what was done in the early days of accounting.

Let us see how transactions are entered in the journal. For this purpose we shall assume that on May 1, 1956, Joseph Burns, a consulting engineer, commenced business with an investment of $5,000.00 in cash, and that during the next few weeks the following transactions took place in his business:

May 2, paid rent for the month of May, $200.00.

May 4, furniture was purchased from the Lincoln Furniture Company on credit for $1,250.00.

May 7, office supplies billed at $72.89 were purchased from R. J. Carter on credit.

23

May 8, services were performed for the Milford Corporation and a bill for $650.00 was sent to them.

May 10, furniture was purchased for $128.75, cash.

May 14, the Milford Corporation paid bill of May 8.

May 15, salaries were paid to the employees for the first half of the month of May. The payroll amounted to $850.00, from which there were deducted $102.10 for federal income taxes withheld and $17.00 for social security taxes under the Federal Insurance Contributions Act. The payroll deductions constitute accounts payable to the Director of Internal Revenue.

May 16, performed services for R. L. Johnson and was paid $450.00 therefor.

May 18, paid R. J. Carter for purchase of May 7.

The following is a chart of the accounts to be used. Note that numbers have been assigned to the accounts.

JOSEPH BURNS
CHART OF ACCOUNTS

Assets

CURRENT ASSETS:
- 1   Cash
-     Accounts receivable
- 10   Milford Corporation

FIXED ASSETS:
- 20   Furniture

Liabilities

CURRENT LIABILITIES:
-     Accounts payable
- 30   R. J. Carter
- 35   Lincoln Furniture Company
- 40   Federal income tax withholdings payable
- 41   F. I. C. A. taxes payable
- 45   Payrolls payable

Capital

- 50   Joseph Burns, Capital

INCOME:
- 60   Income from fees

EXPENSES:
- 72   Office supplies
- 73   Rent
- 75   Salaries

The transactions are entered in the journal as shown on page 25.

Journal

1956 May				
	1	On this day Joseph Burns commenced business as a consulting engineer with the following investment:		
		Cash	5,000.00	
		Joseph Burns, Capital		5,000.00
	2	Rent	200.00	
		Cash		200.00
		Rent for month of May.		
	4	Furniture	1,250.00	
		Lincoln Furniture Company		1,250.00
		Purchased furniture on credit.		
	7	Office supplies	72.89	
		R. J. Carter		72.89
		Purchased office supplies on credit.		
	8	Milford Corporation	650.00	
		Income from fees		650.00
		Performed services for above client.		
	10	Furniture	128.75	
		Cash		128.75
		Purchased furniture for cash.		
	14	Cash	650.00	
		Milford Corporation		650.00
		Received payment of bill of May 8.		
	15	Salaries	850.00	
		Federal income tax withholdings payable		102.10
		F.I.C.A. taxes payable		17.00
		Cash		730.90
		Payroll for first half of May.		
	16	Cash	450.00	
		Income from fees		450.00
		Performed services for R. L. Johnson.		
	18	R. J. Carter	72.89	
		Cash		72.89
		Bill of May 7.		

You will no doubt have observed that in entering transactions in the journal the first two columns are used for the date. The third is used to indicate the accounts to be debited and credited, the name of the account to be debited being inserted at the extreme left and that of the account to be credited indented. Below the titles of the accounts to be debited and credited is written an explanation of the transaction.

At the extreme right are two amount columns, the first for the amounts to be debited and the second for the amounts to be credited.

Between the debit-credit-explanation column and the amount columns is a narrow column called the *posting reference column,* also known as the *ledger folio column.* It will be used when the data are carried to or posted to the ledger.

In opening a new journal a brief description of the business is traditionally given, as shown in the illustration. This is followed by the debits and credits required to record the status of the investment. Such an entry is known as an *opening entry* or *pro forma entry.* Thus in the opening entry the debits and credits follow the description or explanation while in subsequent entries they precede it.

THE CASH RE-CEIPTS BOOK

Although it is possible to operate an accounting system with only one book of original entry, the journal, in most businesses the receipts and disbursements of cash are sufficiently numerous to warrant the use of a special book to record the receipts of cash and one to record the disbursements of cash. These books are the *cash receipts book* and the *cash disbursements book.*

A form for a cash receipts book is illustrated on page 27. In this book are entered the three cash receipts in the business of Joseph Burns mentioned above, namely, his investment of $5,000.00 on May 1, the receipt of $650.00 from the Milford Corporation on May 14, and the receipt of $450.00 from R. L. Johnson on May 16.

Whenever cash is received the asset cash increases and, therefore, the account Cash is to be debited. The corresponding credit will depend on the reason for the receipt of the cash. When cash is received from Joseph Burns as his investment in the business, the account Joseph Burns, Capital is credited. When cash is received from a client in payment of an amount owing, as in the case of the Milford Corporation, the account receivable with that client is credited. And when the cash represents a payment for services performed for a client, as in the case of R. L. Johnson, the account representing the

26

Cash Receipts Book   1

DATE		ACCOUNT CR.	EXPLANATION		AMOUNT CR.	CASH DR.
1956 May	1	Joseph Burns, Capital	Investment	✓	5,000.00	5,000.00
	14	Milford Corporation......................	Bill of May 8	10	650.00	650.00
	16	Income from fees.........................	Services to R. L. Johnson...............	60	450.00	450.00
	31				32,571.80	32,571.80
					(✓)	(1)

particular form of income for which the money is received is credited, in this case Income from Fees. And so forth.

Since the debit for each transaction recorded in the cash receipts book is to Cash, the name of the account to be debited need not be entered as is done when cash receipts are recorded in the journal. Therefore, only the name of the account to be credited is entered.

The cash receipts book is provided with debit and credit columns as in the journal, but these have been reversed so that the amount of cash received may readily be observed at the right end of the page. At the end of each month the amount columns are totaled; and, of course, the totals should be equal. The total of the *cash debit* column will indicate the amount of cash received during the month.

As in the journal, the amount columns are preceded by a posting reference column to be used when the data are posted to the ledger.

The simplification of the entry for each cash receipt, by writing only the name of the account to be credited, reduces the amount of clerical labor. Similar labor-saving takes place in other special books of original entry. It is for this reason that special books of original entry for types of transactions that occur frequently are used instead of recording all transactions in the journal.

Whenever cash is disbursed the asset cash decreases and, there-fore, the account Cash is credited. The corresponding debit will de-pend on the reason for the disbursement. When cash is paid for the acquisition of a fixed asset the account with that asset is debited. When a payment is for an expense the account with the particular form of expense is debited. When cash is paid to a creditor in payment of

THE CASH DIS-BURSEMENTS BOOK

27

Cash Disbursements Book

1

DATE		ACCOUNT DR.	EXPLANATION		AMOUNT DR.	CASH CR.
1956 May	2	Rent	For month of May	73	200.00	200.00
	10	Furniture	Purchased furniture	20	128.75	128.75
	15	Payrolls payable......................	First half of May.....................	45	730.90	730.90
	18	R. J. Carter	Bill of May 7	30	72.89	72.89
	31				26,109.87	26,109.87
					(✓)	(1)

an account payable the account with that creditor is debited. And so forth.

To simplify the recording of cash disbursements a book similar in principle to the cash receipts book is used. Such a book for the business of Joseph Burns is illustrated above. In this book are recorded the four disbursements in our illustrative case. They illustrate the three types of disbursements mentioned above.

You have seen that in the case of each entry in the cash receipts book the debit is to Cash and therefore this fact need not be stated. In similar manner, since for each disbursement of cash the credit is to Cash, only the name of the account to be debited is entered. The amount columns are totaled at the end of each month and the totals of the debit and credit columns should be equal. The total of the *cash credit* column will indicate the amount of cash disbursed during the month.

Having entered the transactions involving the receipt and disbursement of cash in special books for these types of transactions, the entries for the other transactions are made in the journal as shown on page 29.

POSTING

All transactions having been entered in the three books of original entry, they are now posted to the ledger. Each debit and each credit is recorded or posted in the proper account. The fact that the item has been posted is indicated in the posting reference column of the book of original entry by inserting the number of the account to which the debit or credit has been posted, or the number of the page in the ledger on which the account is to be found. Thus, for example,

Journal

1956 May					
	1	On this day Joseph Burns commenced business as a consulting engineer with the following investment:			
		Cash	✓	5,000.00	
		Joseph Burns, Capital	50		5,000.00
	4	Furniture _____..................................	20	1,250.00	
		Lincoln Furniture Company	35		1,250.00
		Purchased furniture on credit.			
	7	Office supplies	72	72.89	
		R. J. Carter	30		72.89
		Purchased office supplies on credit.			
	8	Milford Corporation	10	650.00	
		Income from fees	60		650.00
		Performed services for above client.			
	15	Salaries	75	850.00	
		Federal income tax withholdings payable	40		102.10
		F.I.C.A. taxes payable	41		17.00
		Payrolls payable	45		730.90
		Payroll for first half of May.			

the journal of Joseph Burns shows that the debit of $1,250.00 to Furniture on May 4 has been posted to account No. 20 in the ledger; the cash receipts book shows that the credit of $650.00 to the account of the Milford Corporation has been posted to account No. 10; and the cash disbursements book shows that the debit to Rent of $200.00 has been posted to account No. 73.

In the ledger there are posting reference columns preceding the amount columns in which is inserted a reference to the book of original entry and the page of the book from which each of the postings was made. The posting reference columns thus provide a cross-index: the columns in the books of original entry indicate where the accounts to which the items have been posted may be found in the ledger, and the columns in the ledger show the source of the postings. The insertion of the posting reference numbers in the books of original entry enables one to see at a glance which items have been posted.

Your attention is directed to the fact that the total of the *cash debit* column in the cash receipts book is posted to the debit of the Cash account and this is indicated by writing the posting reference below the amount. Similarly, the total of the *cash credit* column in the cash disbursements book is posted to the credit of the Cash account. The totals of the *credit* column in the cash receipts book and the *debit* column in the cash disbursements book are not posted since the items in these columns are posted individually. The fact that the totals are not to be posted is indicated by a check (✓) below the amounts. The posting of one debit to Cash for the total of the cash received during the month and one credit to Cash for the total of the cash disbursed during the month constitutes another saving of labor by the use of special books of original entry.

You will note that the investment of $5,000.00 on May 1 is entered in both the journal and the cash receipts book. It is entered in the journal because it constitutes the opening entry which is traditionally made in the journal. It is entered in the cash receipts book because it is a cash receipt. However, only one debit and one credit are to be posted: a debit to Cash and a credit to Joseph Burns, Capital. This is achieved by placing a check in the posting reference column of the journal alongside the debit to Cash in order to indicate that this is not to be posted. A similar check is placed in the cash receipts book to indicate that the credit to Joseph Burns, Capital is not to be posted from this book. Thus the debit to Cash will be posted from the cash receipts book, included in the total receipts for the month, and the credit to Joseph Burns, Capital will be posted from the journal.

Also, there are entries in both the journal and the cash disbursements book for the payroll. The entry in the journal records the liability to the Director of Internal Revenue for the federal income taxes withheld and for the social security taxes, and to the employees for their "take home pay." The entry in the cash disbursements book is for the cash paid to the employees. The liability to the Director of Internal Revenue will be paid in due time.

THE LEDGER   After having posted all the transactions of the illustrative case, the ledger of Joseph Burns will appear as shown below.

Ledger

Cash   1

1956						1956					
May	31			CR1	32,571.80	May	31			CD1	26,109.87

Milford Corporation   10

1956 May	8		J1	650.00	1956 May	10		CR1	650.00

Furniture   20

1956 May	4		J1	1,250.00					
	8		CD1	128.75					

R. J. Carter   30

1956 May	18		CD1	72.89	1956 May	7		J1	72.89

Lincoln Furniture Company   35

					1956 May	4		J1	1,250.00

Federal Income Tax Withholdings Payable   40

					1956 May	15		J1	102.10

F.I.C.A. Taxes Payable   41

					1956 May	15		J1	17.00

31

Payrolls Payable   45

1956					1956						
May	15		CD1	730.90	May	15				J1	730.90

Joseph Burns, Capital   50

					1956						
					May	1				J1	5,000.00

Income from Fees   60

					1956						
					May	8				J1	650.00
						15				CR1	450.00

Office Supplies   72

1956											
May	7		J1	72.89							

Rent   73

1956											
May	2		CD1	200.00							

Salaries   75

1956											
May	15		J1	850.00							

32

5. Illustrative Case: Original Entries and Ledger

LET US ASSUME that on June 1, 1956, Thomas Morris commenced business as an efficiency expert engaged in installing business systems and that the financial transactions in his business during the month of June, 1956, were as follows:

1956

June 1—Thomas Morris commenced business with an investment of $7,500.00 in cash.

4—Rent was paid for the month of June, $300.00.

4—Furniture was purchased from the Franklin Furniture Company on credit for $1,357.50.

5—Office supplies billed at $67.58 were purchased from Golding Supply Company on credit.

6—A table was purchased for cash, $85.25.

7—Services were performed for the Atwood Corporation and a bill for $800.00 was sent to them.

8—Services were performed for J. T. Rose for which a non-interest-bearing, 60-day note for $350.00 was received in payment.

11—The Franklin Furniture Company was paid $1,357.50 for the furniture purchased on June 4.

11—Atwood Corporation paid the bill sent them on June 7.

12—William Goodman, to whom services had been rendered, paid immediately, $150.00.

14—Golding Supply Company was paid $67.58 for the office supplies purchased on June 5.

15—Paid the payroll for the first half of June amounting to $940.00, less deductions of $158.50 for federal income taxes withheld, and $18.80 for F.I.C.A. taxes.

15—Thomas Morris withdrew $250.00 for personal use.

18—Services were performed for Charles Reynolds and Company and a bill for $950.00 was sent to them.

20—Miscellaneous expenses amounting to $52.46 were paid for.

20—Postage stamps amounting to $10.50 were purchased.

22—Services were performed for Wood and Adams and a bill for $750.00 was sent to them.

1956

June 26—Charles Reynolds and Company paid the bill sent them on June 18.

27—Services were performed for Atwood Corporation and a bill for $436.00 was sent to them.

28—Purchased furniture from Franklin Furniture Company on credit for $325.00.

28—Purchased office supplies from Golding Supply Company on credit for $63.87.

29—Paid the payroll for the second half of June amounting to $940.00, less deductions of $158.50 for federal income taxes withheld, and $18.80 for F.I.C.A. taxes.

29—Services were performed for Fred Singer and a bill for $225.00 was sent to him.

The chart of accounts of the business of Thomas Morris is found on page 35, the books of original entry on pages 36—37, and the ledger on pages 38—41.

THOMAS MORRIS
CHART OF ACCOUNTS

Assets

CURRENT ASSETS:

- 1 Cash
- 5 Notes receivable
  Accounts receivable
- 20 Atwood Corporation
- 25 Charles Reynolds and Company
- 27 Fred Singer
- 29 Wood and Adams

FIXED ASSETS:

- 40 Furniture

Liabilities

CURRENT LIABILITIES:

Accounts payable
- 65 Franklin Furniture Company
- 68 Golding Supply Company
- 90 Federal income tax withholdings payable
- 91 F.I.C.A. taxes payable
- 95 Payrolls payable

Capital

- 100 Thomas Morris, Capital
- 101 Thomas Morris, Drawing

INCOME:

- 120 Income from fees

EXPENSES:

- 150 Rent
- 153 Salaries
- 156 Office supplies
- 157 Postage
- 158 Miscellaneous expense

35

Journal

1

1956						
June	1	On this day Thomas Morris commenced business as an efficiency expert with the following investment: Cash		7,500.00		
		Thomas Morris, Capital	100			7,500.00
	4	Furniture	40	1,357.50		
		Franklin Furniture Company	65			1,357.50
		Purchased furniture on credit.				
	5	Office supplies ....,......................................	156	67.58		
		Golding Supply Company	68			67.58
		Purchased office supplies on credit.				
	7	Atwood Corporation	20	800.00		
		Income from fees	120			800.00
		Performed services for above client.				
	8	Notes receivable	5	350.00		
		Income from fees	120			350.00
		Performed services for J. T. Rose and received a non-interest-bearing, 60-day note in payment.				
	15	Salaries	153	940.00		
		Federal income tax withholdings payable	90			158.50
		F.I.C.A. taxes payable	91			18.80
		Payrolls payable	95			762.70
		Payroll for first half of June.				
	18	Charles Reynolds and Company	25	950.00		
		Income from fees...	120			950.00
		Performed services for above client.				
	22	Wood and Adams	29	750.00		
		Income from fees	120			750.00
		Performed services for above client.				
	27	Atwood Corporation	20	436.00		
		Income from fees	120			436.00
		Performed services for above client.				
	28	Furniture	40	325.00		
		Franklin Furniture Company	65			325.00
		Purchased furniture on credit.				
		Carried forward		13,476.08		13,476.08

Journal 2

		Brought forward		13,476.08	13,476.08
1956 June	28	Office supplies	156	63.87	
		Golding Supply Company	68		63.87
		Purchased office supplies on credit.			
	29	Salaries	153	940.00	
		Federal income tax withholdings payable	90		158.50
		F.I.C.A. taxes payable	91		18.80
		Payrolls payable	95		762.70
		Payroll for second half of June.			
	29	Fred Singer	27	225.00	
		Income from fees	120		225.00
		Performed services for above client.			
				14,704.95	14,704.95

Cash Receipts Book 1

DATE		ACCOUNT CR.	EXPLANATION		AMOUNT CR.	CASH DR.
1956 June	1	Thomas Morris, Capital	Investment	✓	7,500.00	7,500.00
	11	Atwood Corporation	Bill of June 7	20	800.00	800.00
	12	Income from fees..........................	William Goodman paid fee	120	150.00	150.00
	26	Charles Reynolds and Company	Bill of June 18	25	950.00	950.00
	30				9,400.00	9,400.00
					(✔)	(1)

Cash Disbursements Book 1

DATE		ACCOUNT DR.	EXPLANATION		AMOUNT DR.	CASH CR.
1956 June	4	Rent	Month of June	150	300.00	300.00
	6	Furniture	Purchased table	40	85.25	85.25
	11	Franklin Furniture Company	Bill of June 4	65	1,357.50	1,357.50
	14	Golding Supply Company	Bill of June 5	68	67.58	67.58
	15	Payrolls payable.........................	First half of June	95	762.70	762.70
	15	Thomas Morris, Drawing	Withdrawal	101	250.00	250.00
	20	Miscellaneous expense	....	158	52.46	52.46
	20	Postage	Purchased stamps.........................	157	10.50	10.50
	29	Payrolls payable.........................	Second half of June	95	762.70	762.70
	30				3,648.69	3,648.69
					(✔)	(1)

Ledger

Cash   1

1956					1956				
June	30	5,751.31	CR1	9,400.00	June	30		CD1	3,648.69

Notes Receivable   5

1956				
June	8	J1		350.00

Atwood Corporation   20

1956					1956				
June	7		J1	800.00	June	11		CR1	800.00
	27	436.00	J2	436.00					
				1,236.30					

Charles Reynolds and Company   25

1956					1956				
June	18	J1	950.00	June	26		CR1	950.00

Fred Singer   27

1956				
June	29	J2	225.00

Wood and Adams 29

1956				
June	22		J1	750.00

Furniture 40

1956				
June	2		J1	1,357.50
	28		J2	325.00
	6		CD1	85.25
				1,767.75

Franklin Furniture Company 65

1956				1956				
June	11		CD1	1,357.50	June	2		J1	1,357.50
						28	325.00	J2	325.00
									1,682.50

Golding Supply Company 68

1956				1956				
June	14		CD1	67.58	June	5		J1	67.58
						28	63.87	J2	63.87
									131.45

Federal Income Tax Withholdings Payable 90

				1956				
				June	15		J1	158.50
					29		J2	158.50
								317.00

39

F.I.C.A. Taxes Payable   91

					1956				
					June	15		J1	18.80
						29		J2	18.80
									3 7.6 0

Payrolls Payable   95

1956					1956				
June	15		CD1	762.70	June	15		J1	762.70
	29		CD1	762.70		29		J2	762.70
				1,5 2 5.4 0					1,5 2 5.4 0

Thomas Morris, Capital   100

					1956				
					June	1		J1	7,500.00

Thomas Morris, Drawing   101

1956									
June	15		CD1	250.00					

Income from Fees   120

					1956				
					June	7		J1	800.00
						8		J1	350.00
						18		J1	950.00
						22		J1	750.00
						27		J1	436.00
						29		J2	225.00
						12		CR1	150.00
									3,6 6 1.0 0

Rent — 150

1956									
June	4		CD1	300.00					

Salaries — 153

1956									
June	15		J1	940.00					
	29		J2	940.00					
				1,880.00					

Office Supplies — 156

1956									
June	5		J1	67.58					
	28		J2	63.87					
				131.45					

Postage — 157

1956									
June	20		CD1	10.50					

Miscellaneous Expense — 158

1956									
June	20		CD1	52.46					

41

6. The Trial Balance

SINCE THE accounting record of every business transaction consists of a debit and a credit element which are equal, it follows that the total of all the debits posted into the ledger in a given period of time will be equal to the total of all the credits posted therein.

A list of the totals of the debits and credits in each account in the ledger of Thomas Morris, the illustrative case of Chapter 5, follows. It is seen that the total of the debits in the ledger is equal to the total of the credits; and this is what we expect to find.

	Debits	Credits
Cash	$ 9,400.00	$ 3,648.69
Notes receivable	350.00	
Atwood Corporation	1,236.00	800.00
Charles Reynolds and Company	950.00	950.00
Fred Singer	225.00	
Wood and Adams	750.00	
Furniture	1,767.75	
Franklin Furniture Company	1,357.50	1,682.50
Golding Supply Company	67.58	131.45
Federal income tax withholdings payable		317.00
F.I.C.A. taxes payable		37.60
Payrolls payable	1,525.40	1,525.40
Thomas Morris, Capital		7,500.00
Thomas Morris, Drawing	250.00	
Income from fees		3,661.00
Rent	300.00	
Salaries	1,880.00	
Office supplies	131.45	
Postage	10.50	
Miscellaneous expense	52.46	
	$20,253.64	$20,253.64

If, instead of tabulating the total debits and credits in the accounts, the balances of the accounts are listed, it will be found that the total of the debit balances is equal to the total of the credit balances.

The following are the balances of the accounts in the ledger of Thomas Morris:

	Debit Balances	Credit Balances
Cash	$ 5,751.31	
Notes receivable	350.00	
Atwood Corporation	436.00	
Fred Singer	225.00	
Wood and Adams	750.00	
Furniture	1,767.75	
Franklin Furniture Company		$ 325.00
Golding Supply Company		63.87
Federal income tax withholdings payable		317.00
F.I.C.A. taxes payable		37.60
Thomas Morris, Capital		7,500.00
Thomas Morris, Drawing	250.00	
Income from fees		3,661.00
Rent	300.00	
Salaries	1,880.00	
Office supplies	131.45	
Postage	10.50	
Miscellaneous expense	52.46	
	$11,904.47	$11,904.47

The balance of each account is the difference when the total of the lesser side is deducted from that of the greater. The same figure is obtained by deducting the amount of the lesser side from the amount of each side; and since when equals are deducted from equals the differences are equal, the equality of debits and credits is maintained.

For example, in our illustrative case the total of the lesser or credit side of the Cash account is $3,648.69. Deducting this amount from the total of the debit side, $9,400.00, leaves the debit balance of $5,751.31. Deducting $3,648.69 from both the debit side and the credit side yields the equivalent result: $5,751.31 on the debit side and 0 on the credit side.

Such a tabulation, as has been given above, of either the footings of the two sides of each account or the balances of the accounts is called a *trial balance* because it is a trial or test of the equality of the debits and credits in the ledger, or what might be called the "equilibrium" of the ledger. A test of this sort is necessary from time to time to determine whether the debits and credits in the ledger are equal, as required by the rules of accounting.

Either of the two methods illustrated might be employed, but the method in common use is the second: that which uses the balances of the accounts. A list of account balances is most useful because it shows the position of each account at the time the trial balance is made.

It is customary for the accountant to compile or *take off* a trial balance at the end of each month in order to be certain that the ledger is in balance before he begins to post the items of the following month.

From the fact that a trial balance balances it does not necessarily follow that all of the postings are correct. An error might have been made in posting that did not affect the equality of debits and credits. Such error might be made by posting a debit or credit to a wrong account, or by completely neglecting to post a certain transaction. Also, compensating errors in addition or subtraction might have been made when footing the accounts or computing the balances; that is, an error of like amount might have been made on both the debit and credit side. Because such errors are not brought to light by the use of a trial balance, they will have to be discovered in other ways. For example, an error in an account receivable would be discovered when a statement of his account is sent to a customer.

TRIAL BALANCE OUT OF BALANCE

When the total of the debit balances in a trial balance does not equal the total of the credit balances, it is said to be *out of balance*. This indicates the existence of one or more errors; and such error or errors must be discovered and corrected before the transactions of the next month are posted.

A starting point is to determine the amount of difference between the debit and credit balances. This will often give a clue, for the difference may be the exact amount of an unposted item. Also, if there is a difference of 1 in any column, the error may have been made in addition.

If the discrepancy is not revealed by the amount of the difference, it will be necessary to check the work. The preferable procedure in locating errors is to check backward from the trial balance to the entries in the books of original entry. A suggested sequence is to check: (1) the addition of the trial balance; (2) the account balances in the trial balance with those in the ledger; (3) the addition and subtraction in the accounts; (4) the postings from the books of original entry to the ledger; (5) the additions and entries in the books of original entry.

7. Subsidiary Ledgers

THERE ARE USUALLY two groups of accounts in the ledger that tend to become very large in comparison with the rest of the accounts. These are the accounts receivable and the accounts payable. In fact, in some businesses they outnumber the rest of the accounts many thousandfold. Therefore, in order to facilitate the handling of the accounts, these two groups are placed in separate ledgers called the *accounts receivable ledger* (also known as the *customers'* or *sales ledger*) and the *accounts payable ledger* (also known as the *creditors'* or *purchases ledger*).

NEED FOR SUB-
DIVISION OF
THE LEDGER

The accounts receivable and accounts payable ledgers may be subdivided further into several volumes. As the accounts in these ledgers are usually arranged alphabetically, one volume might contain, for example, accounts with names beginning with the letters *A* to *E*, the next with letters *F* to *K*, and so on. By thus dividing the accounts receivable and accounts payable ledgers into a number of volumes, several clerks may at one time be engaged in posting to them.

Placing the accounts receivable and the accounts payable in separate ledgers in no way changes the status of these accounts in the accounting system. The accounts receivable are still current assets and the accounts payable current liabilities. It is an arrangement for convenience. And in order to maintain the equality of debits and credits in the general ledger the accounts receivable and the accounts payable are each represented in this ledger by a single account named respectively Accounts Receivable and Accounts Payable. These accounts are called *control accounts*.

SUBSIDIARY
LEDGERS AND
CONTROL AC-
COUNTS

The postings are made to the customers' and creditors' accounts from day to day in the manner already explained. The postings to the control accounts, however, are made at the end of each month from totals of certain columns which are inserted in the books of original entry for the purpose of accumulating these data. As a result, when all the postings have been made for any month, the debit balance in the Accounts Receivable control account in the general ledger should equal the total of the balances of the accounts in the accounts receivable ledger. Similarly, the credit balance in the Accounts Payable control should equal the total of the balances of the accounts in the accounts payable ledger.

The separate ledgers for accounts receivable and accounts payable are thus tied to the general ledger by means of the control accounts and have a subordinate position to that ledger. They are accordingly known as *subsidiary ledgers*. The control accounts have been so called since the balances of these accounts agree with or control the total of the balances in the subsidiary ledgers.

Let us now examine forms for the books of original entry when subsidiary ledgers for the accounts receivable and the accounts payable are employed.

THE CASH RE-CEIPTS BOOK

Continuing the illustrative case of Thomas Morris, a form for the cash receipts book, if subsidiary ledgers are used for the accounts receivable and the accounts payable, is shown on page 47. There has been inserted in this form an *accounts receivable ledger credit* column in which each payment by a customer is entered. These amounts are posted to the credit of the customers from whom the remittances have been received in the accounts receivable ledger. At the end of each month the total of the *accounts receivable ledger credit* column is posted to the credit of the Accounts Receivable control account in the general ledger. The total of the *general ledger credit* column is not posted, as indicated.

You will observe that the Accounts Receivable control has been assigned account No. 10. Also that since the accounts in the subsidiary ledger will be placed in alphabetical order rather than being assigned numbers, postings are indicated by a tick (ᨆ) instead of account numbers.

THE CASH DIS-BURSEMENTS BOOK

A form for the cash disbursements book of Thomas Morris, if subsidiary ledgers for the accounts receivable and the accounts payable are used, is also illustrated on page 47. There has been inserted an *accounts payable ledger debit* column in which each payment to a creditor is entered. These amounts are posted to the debit of the creditors to whom the remittances have been made, in the accounts payable ledger. At the end of each month the total of the *accounts payable ledger debit* column is posted to the debit of the Accounts Payable control account in the general ledger, which account has been

Cash Receipts Book

1

DATE		ACCOUNT CR.	EXPLANATION		GENERAL LEDGER CR.	ACCOUNTS REC. LEDGER CR.	CASH DR.
1956 June							
	1	Thomas Morris, Capital	Investment	✓	7,500.00		7,500.00
	11	Atwood Corporation	Bill of June 7	✓		800.00	800.00
	12	Income from fees	William Goodman paid fee	✓	150.00		150.00
	26	Charles Reynolds and Company	Bill of June 18			950.00	950.00
	30				7,650.00	1,750.00	9,400.00
					(✓)	(10)	(1)

Cash Disbursements Book

1

DATE		ACCOUNT DR.	EXPLANATION	GENERAL LEDGER DR.	ACCOUNTS PAY. LEDGER DR.	CASH CR.
1956 June						
	4	Rent	Month of June	300.00		300.00
	6	Furniture	Purchased table	85.25		85.25
	11	Franklin Furniture Company	Bill of June 4		1,357.50	1,357.50
	14	Golding Supply Company	Bill of June 5		67.58	67.58
	15	Payrolls payable	First half of June		762.70	762.70
	15	Thomas Morris, Drawing	Withdrawal	250.00		250.00
	20	Miscellaneous expense		52.46		52.46
	20	Postage	Purchased stamps	10.50		10.50
	29	Payrolls payable	Second half of June		762.70	762.70
	30			698.21	2,950.48	3,648.69
				(✓)	(60)	(1)

Journal

Accounts Payable Ledger (Dr)	Accounts Rec'able Ledger (Dr)	General Ledger (Dr)		General Ledger (Cr)	Accounts Rec'able Ledger (Cr)	Accounts Payable Ledger (Cr)
			June 1, 1956			
			On this day Thomas Morris commenced business as an efficiency expert with the following investment:			
		7,500.00	Cash .... ✓			
			Thomas Morris, Capital	7,500.00		
			2			
		1,357.50	Furniture			
			Franklin Furniture Company			1,357.50
			Purchased furniture on credit.			
			5			
		67.58	Office supplies			
			Golding Supply Company			67.58
			Purchased office supplies on credit.			
			7			
	800.00		Atwood Corporation			
			Income from fees	800.00		
			Performed services for above client.			
			8			
		350.00	Notes receivable			
			Income from fees	350.00		
			Performed services for J. T. Rose and received a non-interest-bearing, 60-day note in payment.			
			15			
		940.00	Salaries.......................................			
			Federal income tax withholdings payable....			158.50
			F.I.C.A. taxes payable..................			18.80
			Payrolls payable........................			762.70
			Payroll for first half of June.			
			18			
	950.00		Charles Reynolds and Company			
			Income from fees	950.00		
			Performed services for above client.			
			22			
	750.00		Wood and Adams			
			Income from fees	750.00		
			Performed services for above client.			

Account / Explanation				
27				
Atwood Corporation	436.00			
Income from fees				436.00
Performed services for above client.				
28				
Furniture		325.00	325.00	
Franklin Furniture Company				
Purchased furniture on credit.				
28				
Office supplies		63.87	63.87	
Golding Supply Company				
Purchased office supplies on credit.				
29				
Salaries		940.00		
Federal income tax withholdings payable			158.50	
F.I.C.A. taxes payable			18.80	
Payrolls payable			762.70	
Payroll for second half of June.				
29				
Fred Singer	225.00			
Income from fees				225.00
Performed services for above client.				
	3,161.00	11,543.95	3,693.95	11,011.00
	(10)	(✓)	(60)	(✓)

given No. 60. As in the case of the cash receipts book, the total of the *general ledger debit* column is not posted.

THE JOURNAL   A form for the journal of Thomas Morris, if subsidiary ledgers are used for the accounts receivable and the accounts payable, is shown on pages 48–49. Since the subsidiary ledger system may require a debit or credit to be posted to any one of three different ledgers, the debits and credits are classified in three different columns, thus making six in all. Because in this form the debit-credit-explanation column is placed in the middle, it is known as the *six-column divided journal*.

The debits and credits are posted as usual from day to day to the respective ledgers. At the end of each month the totals of the *accounts receivable ledger* and the *accounts payable ledger* columns are posted to the respective control accounts in the general ledger. The totals of the *general ledger* columns are, of course, not posted.

By following the procedure here outlined, we achieve the objective mentioned at the beginning of this chapter: that the balances in the control accounts will at the end of each month equal the totals of the balances of the accounts in the subsidiary ledgers.

THE TRIAL
BALANCE   After having posted all transactions, the trial balance of the general ledger of Thomas Morris as of June 30, 1956, will appear as follows:

Cash	$ 5,751.31	
Notes receivable	350.00	
Accounts receivable	1,411.00	
Furniture	1,767.75	
Accounts payable		$ 743.47
Thomas Morris, Capital		7,500.00
Thomas Morris, Drawing	250.00	
Income from fees		3,661.00
Rent	300.00	
Salaries	1,880.00	
Office supplies	131.45	
Postage	10.50	
Miscellaneous expense	52.46	
	$11,904.47	$11,904.47

The only difference between this trial balance and the trial balance in Chapter 6 is that, instead of containing the balances of each of the accounts receivable and the accounts payable, it contains the balances of the Accounts Receivable and Accounts Payable control accounts. These accounts appear in the general ledger as follows:

50

Accounts Receivable 10

1956 June	30		1,411.00	J1	3,161.00	1956 June	30			CR1	1,750.00

Accounts Payable 60

1956 June	30			CD1	2,950.48	1956 June	30		743.47	J1	3,693.95

The trial balance of a subsidiary ledger is made by balancing the total of the account balances in the ledger against the balance of the control account.

The following is the trial balance of the accounts receivable ledger of Thomas Morris as of June 30, 1956:

Atwood Corporation	$ 436.00	
Fred Singer	225.00	
Wood and Adams	750.00	
Accounts receivable control		$1,411.00
	$1,411.00	$1,411.00

The trial balance of the accounts payable ledger is:

Accounts payable control	$ 743.47	
Franklin Furniture Company		$ 325.00
Golding Supply Company		63.87
Federal income tax withholdings payable		317.00
F.I.C.A. taxes payable		37.60
	$ 743.47	$ 743.47

It is seen from the above trial balances that a system of subsidiary ledgers with control accounts in the general ledger provides a check on the accounts in the subsidiary ledgers since the data in the control accounts, compiled independently, must agree with those in the subsidiary ledgers.

OTHER SUBSIDIARY LEDGERS

The use of subsidiary ledgers is not limited to accounts receivable and accounts payable. There is no assignable limit to the number of subsidiary ledgers that a business may use. This device is

51

useful in facilitating the keeping of any group of accounts that tends to become large. In some enterprises a subsidiary ledger is used for buildings and equipment. In this are found accounts for each type of fixed asset. Large corporations use a subsidiary ledger to keep accounts showing the investment of each of the stockholders, in which case the Capital Stock account is the control account.

8. Cash Control

THE ITEM *cash* in the accounting records may include not only currency subject to immediate use but also uncollected checks. These checks, for practical purposes, are considered the equivalent of cash since they will be collected within a few days by the bank and thus be converted into available funds.

Besides cash immediately available, or almost so, a business may possess cash that is not subject to immediate use such as time deposits that may not be withdrawn until a certain number of days have elapsed after notice to the bank. It may also own cash that is restricted in its use, such as cash set aside for the payment of employees' pensions, or cash that is in a closed bank. Such cash not available for use in the operation of the business is segregated in the accounts.

Because of its desirability and its ease of misappropriation it is essential to exercise rigid control over cash. Fortunately it is an asset that it is possible to handle and to record with precision.

To control the receipt and disbursement of cash it is necessary to have an adequate system of *internal check*. By internal check is meant an arrangement by which the various functions to be performed are so distributed among the employees that the work of one serves to verify that of another. The distribution of the functions and the extent to which they are segregated will obviously depend on the size of the organization.

The basic separation of functions in the case of cash is that of having the cash books kept by a person other than those who actually handle the cash. A suggested arrangement for the control of receipts is to place a clerk in charge of all cash received; he compiles a memorandum record of the incoming checks and of cash register receipts. The record is turned over to the clerk in charge of the cash books, who may be known as the bookkeeper, while the cash itself is turned over to a third person, who may be called the cashier, and whose function it is to make the deposits.

53

The cashier should deposit all receipts in the bank on the day they are received, if possible. He prepares for this purpose a form supplied by the bank known as a *deposit slip* on which are tabulated the amounts of the checks and of any currency deposited. The total of the deposit is entered in the *pass book* of the business by the teller receiving the deposit. However, a duplicate deposit slip may be used in place of a pass book and upon making the deposit this duplicate deposit slip is receipted by the teller. In any event, a duplicate slip should be prepared as the cashier's record of the deposit. It is then checked by both the receipts clerk and the bookkeeper.

The reader has been shown how cash receipts are recorded in the cash receipts book. This should be done as soon as possible after the cash is received because the prompt recording of receipts will diminish the possibility of embezzlement. The receipts clerk and the cashier should not have access to the books of account.

CONTROL OF DISBURSEMENTS

The control of disbursements is just as important as the control of receipts. All disbursements should be made by check and supervised by some person appointed for that purpose. It should be his duty to approve and sign the checks for payment after checking the papers submitted to him that show the reason for the disbursement. As an additional safeguard a second person may be designated to countersign the checks. Those who approve checks for payment should not have authority to make entries in the cash books.

THE BANK RECONCILIATION

The fundamental principle of cash control, as outlined above, is that all receipts are deposited in the bank and all disbursements are made by check through the bank. Thus the bank, an independent organization, acts in the capacity of keeping a record of the receipts and disbursements. This serves as an additional check on the records of the business.

At the end of each month the bank submits a statement tabulating all the receipts and disbursements and this is then used to verify the entries in the cash books. With its statement the bank returns all the checks that have been paid during the month, duly canceled, and other papers that explain the items listed in the statement.

It is usually not to be expected that the closing balance shown in the bank statement will agree with the balance indicated by the cash books. There are several reasons for this. If the business has issued checks on the last day of the month it is unlikely that they have been paid by the bank on that day. These checks have been entered in the cash disbursements book and so deducted from the balance according to the books; but they have not been deducted from the bank's balance. Also, receipts may have been recorded in the cash receipts book but not deposited in the bank on the same day. This would be the usual situation when the business deposits its funds with a bank in another city.

On the other hand, the bank may have credited the account of the business for such matters as collections and may have debited it for various charges; and although the bank notified the business at the time by means of *credit* or *debit slips,* these may have been overlooked and the entries not made. Thus it is necessary to reconcile the balance shown by the bank's statement with the balance of the cash books.

Let it be assumed that John White received from the Exchange Bank the statement as of December 31, 1956 illustrated below. This **ILLUSTRATIVE CASE**

EXCHANGE BANK

IN
ACCOUNT
WITH

Mr. John White
325 Main Street
City

LST - List   DM - Debit Memo
CC - Certified Check   EX - Exchange
CM - Credit Memo   SC - Service Charge

DATE	CHECKS CHARGED TO YOUR ACCOUNT—READ ACROSS		DEPOSITS		DATE	BALANCE
	YOUR FORMER BALANCE →				NOV 30'56	3,097.63
DEC 3'56	250.00	18.95	DEC 3'56	847.60	DEC 3'56	3,676.28*
DEC 4'56	1,500.00				DEC 4'56	2,176.28*
			DEC 5 CM	2,852.85	DEC 5'56	5,029.13*
DEC 7'56	14.87	485.96			DEC 7'56	4,528.30*
DEC 11'56	325.00				DEC 11'56	4,203.30*
DEC 12'56	750.00	1,250.00			DEC 12'56	2,203.30*
DEC 26'56	258.75	872.00	DEC 26'56	3,850.00	DEC 26'56	8,241.53*
DEC 27 DM	.25		DEC 27'56	150.00	DEC 27'56	8,391.28*
DEC 28'56	87.90	739.40			DEC 28'56	7,563.98*
DEC 31'56	1,250.00				DEC 31'56	6,313.98*

THIS STATEMENT IS RENDERED UPON CUSTOMERS REQUEST, AND WILL BE READY FOR DELIVERY THE SECOND FOLLOWING BUSINESS DAY.

IF NO ERROR IS REPORTED WITHIN TEN DAYS, THE ACCOUNT WILL BE CONSIDERED CORRECT.

THE LAST AMOUNT IN THIS COLUMN IS YOUR BALANCE.

CHECKS CHARGED ON STATEMENT AND VOUCHERS COMPARED

statement shows a balance of $6,313.98. However, upon referring to the books it was found that the balance there indicated was only $3,190.17.

Arranging the checks returned with the bank statement in numerical order disclosed that the following had not been paid: No. 8762, $152.89; No. 8785, $1,250.00; No. 8788, $18.72; No. 8789, $136.50.

It was also found that receipts totaling $1,286.90 were entered in the cash receipts book but not deposited until January 2, 1957.

Further, it was discovered that the credit of $2,852.85 on December 5 represented the collection of a note receivable which was not recorded in the cash receipts; also that the debit of December 27 for $.25, representing a collection charge, was not entered.

The above discrepancies may be tabulated in a reconciliation of the bank balance with the balance of the cash books in the following manner:

```
Balance per bank statement...........................................................  $6,313.98
Add receipts not deposited until January 2..................................   1,286.90
                                                                               $7,600.88
Deduct outstanding checks:
       No. 8762          $   152.89
          8785            1,250.00
          8788               18.72
          8789              136.50                                              1,558.11
          Correct balance...............................................................  $6,042.77


Balance per books......................................................................  $3,190.17
Add note receivable collected .................................................   2,852.85
                                                                               $6,043.02
Deduct collection charges..........................................................         .25
          Correct balance...............................................................  $6,042.77
```

It is seen that this reconciliation has two parts, each commencing with one of the two balances—the balance per bank statement and the balance per books. Each balance has added to it or subtracted from it those transactions that occurred but were not taken into consideration in arriving at that balance. The result in each section is the correct or "true" balance, that is, the balance that would appear in both the bank statement and in the cash books if both the bank and the business had made entries for all the events that had occurred.

Since the correct balance should appear in the books, it is necessary to make entries to include the missing items therein. In the illustrative case entries would be made in the cash receipts book to record the collection of the note on December 5 and in the cash disburse-

56

ments book to record the collection charge on December 27. In journal form these entries are, respectively:

Cash 2,852.85
     Notes receivable 2,852.85

and:

Miscellaneous expense .... .25
     Cash .... .25

A CONVENTION FOR CONVENIENCE

The above entries would in practice be made in the cash receipts book and cash disbursements book, respectively. However, to simplify discussions of principle as this, it has become customary among accountants, as a matter of convenience, to write entries in journal form. This avoids the obvious difficulty of reproducing the various books of original entry involved in a particular transaction. Such practice will be followed throughout the rest of this book.

PETTY CASH FUND

It has been stated above that all disbursements should be made by check. This, however, is not feasible in instances in which the amount to be paid is very small as, for example, when an employee is paid carfare or when small quantities of postage stamps are purchased. For this purpose it is commonly the practice to keep available in the business a small amount of cash known as the *petty cash fund*.

The usual procedure in handling the petty cash is to appoint someone, who may be called the petty cashier, to take charge of the fund which is established by drawing a check payable to the order of the petty cashier or to "petty cash" for such round sum as is adequate for the needs of the business. The petty cashier cashes the check and keeps the money available for making payments. Such procedure is known as the *imprest* petty cash method. The word "imprest" is here used in the sense of a prepayment of money.

Whenever a small disbursement is necessary the money is paid out by the petty cashier, but only upon obtaining a receipt or *petty cash voucher* for which a special form may be provided requiring an explanation of the disbursement and perhaps approval by someone in charge. The petty cashier places the receipts on file since they vouch for his payments from the fund. At any time the total of the receipts plus the total of the cash on hand should equal the figure at which the fund was established.

When the fund approaches exhaustion the petty cashier prepares a *petty cash statement* in which his disbursements are tabulated. A form for such a statement is shown on page 59. In this form columns are provided for the amounts to be debited to accounts commonly debited with petty expenditures, the total of each column indicating the total debit to some account. At the extreme right end of the statement there is provided a column for the items to be debited to accounts other than those for which special columns are provided. The total of this *sundry accounts* column is analyzed for the purpose of summarization.

The petty cash statement may be prepared on loose sheets or it may be in a book known as the *petty cash book*. A popular arrangement is to have a book with alternate pages of white and yellow paper. When entries are made, a sheet of carbon paper is inserted between the white and yellow pages. The white pages which are used for the original copy are perforated at the left end. When all entries have been made the white pages are torn out and presented to the person in charge of disbursements together with the petty cash vouchers. The yellow pages which bear carbon copies of the data on the white pages are retained in the book as the petty cashier's record of his payments out of the fund.

Upon receiving a petty cash statement showing the amount paid out of the fund, the person in charge of disbursements checks it and if found to be in order has a check prepared for the petty cashier in the amount of the payments made from the fund. This replenishes the fund to its original amount and the petty cashier is ready to make payments again. Thus, although made in cash the payments out of the petty cash fund are ultimately covered by a check paid by the bank.

When the check drawn to establish the petty cash fund is entered in the cash disbursements book the debit for this disbursement is to an account entitled Petty Cash. However, when the fund is replenished the debit is to the various accounts for which payments were made from the petty cash fund as indicated by the petty cash statement. The debit balance in the Petty Cash account remains unchanged unless the fund is either increased or decreased. If the fund is increased the entry is the same as for its establishment; if it is to be decreased the petty cashier turns in the cash representing the decrease and the entry consists of a debit to Cash and a credit to Petty Cash.

Petty Cash

DATE	VOU. NO.	TO WHOM PAID	TOTAL	OFFICE EXPENSE	SALES EXPENSE	SUPPLIES	POSTAGE	SUNDRY ACCOUNTS	
								NAME	AMOUNT
1956 Mar.									
1	1	M. J. Smith	7.50	7.50					
1	2	Postman	.03				.03		
2	3	Railway Express	3.75					Delivery expense	3.75
2	4	Postmaster	15.00				15.00		
3	5	K. G. Peters	32.50			32.50			
4	6	Loxit Corp.	25.00		25.00				
4	7	Henry Garrison	.83	.83					
7	8	O. K. Furniture Co.	18.75					Office furniture	18.75
7	9	Wood Bros.	20.00			20.00			
7	10	Red Cross (Donation)	5.00	5.00					
8	11	Henry Garrison	8.40	8.40					
8	12	P. Robinson	12.50		12.50				
			149.26	21.73	37.50	52.50	15.03		22.50

9. Notes and Drafts

USE OF NOTES A NOTE MAY be required by the seller of merchandise or services because he regards the customer or client as a poor credit risk, the note giving him positive evidence of the debt. But in certain industries, such as lumber and jewelry, payment by note is customary. Notes are also frequently given when purchases are made on the installment plan, a series of notes being drawn, each of which matures at the date when an installment is due. To the seller a note is a note receivable (an asset) and to the buyer it is a note payable (a liability).

Notes are also given in payment of sums of money owing on account. This usually is done when an account becomes due and the debtor is unable to make payment in cash.

A further use of notes is in the borrowing of money. The borrower in such case gives a note to the lender as evidence of the loan. It is customary in the United States for a borrower from a bank to give the bank a note when receiving a loan.

The person who creates the note is known as the *maker* and the person to whom it is to be paid is known as the *payee*.

ENDORSEMENT The usual promissory note is a form of negotiable instrument, that is, it has the quality of being legally transferable from one holder to another. In order to possess negotiability an instrument must be in writing and (1) be signed by the person who creates it, (2) contain an unconditional promise or order to pay a specified sum of money, (3) be payable on demand or at a fixed or determinable time, and (4) be payable to bearer or to the order of a specified payee.

The transfer of ownership of a negotiable instrument is performed by *endorsement;* that is, by the owner signing his name on the back. When he has endorsed the instrument he is known as the *endorser.*

There are several forms of endorsement in use, the two most commonly used being the *blank endorsement* and the *full* or *special endorsement.* The blank endorsement consists of merely the signature of the endorser. When so endorsed the instrument may be collected by the holder thereof in due course. The full endorsement makes the

60

instrument payable to the order of a specific person known as the *endorsee,* and in this form of endorsement the signature of the endorser is preceded by the words "Pay to the order of" and the name of the endorsee. When so endorsed the instrument may be collected only by the endorsee, unless he further endorses it.

If at the maturity date a note should not be paid or *honored* by the maker, it is said to be *dishonored,* and the endorsers are liable for payment.

Notes may bear interest or they may be non-interest-bearing. When notes are given in settlement of accounts they usually bear interest in order to compensate the creditor for waiting for his money in excess of the terms granted when the sale was made.

INTEREST ON NOTES

As defined by economists, interest is a payment for the use of money. When a creditor has to wait for some money owing to him he is entitled to interest on this money since some other person has the use of the money that should be in his possession.

Interest is the product of principal, rate, and time. In the case of a note the principal is the amount stated in the note, known as the *face* of the note, the rate is the specified or, if not specified, the legal rate of interest in the jurisdiction concerned, and the time is the number of days or months from the date of the note to the date of maturity.

The time of a note is most commonly expressed in terms of days and the maturity date is determined by counting the exact number of days from the date the note bears. In counting the days, from the date of the note to the next day is one day, and so on. That is, the days are counted beginning with the day after that borne by the note. Thus, a 30-day note dated March 16 would fall due on April 15.

DETERMINING THE MATURITY DATE

When a note is stated in terms of months, its maturity date is determined by counting the months from the date it bears. Thus, a one-month note dated March 16 would fall due on April 16.

The interest on interest-bearing notes is paid at maturity together with the face of the note. Such interest is a form of expense to the maker and a form of income to the payee. In accounting for notes, therefore, the interest paid on the notes payable of a business is debited to the account Interest Expense, while the interest collected on the notes receivable is credited to the account Interest Income.

ACCOUNTING FOR NOTES AND INTEREST THEREON

61

Thus, when a 60-day note for $500.00 bearing interest at 6 per cent is received from T. J. Larsen, a customer, the entry is:

```
Notes receivable ................................................................... 500.00
      T. J. Larsen (an account receivable)......................          500.00
```

When Larsen pays the note, the entry is:

```
Cash ............................................................................... 505.00
      Notes receivable.......................................................          500.00
      Interest income ........................................................            5.00
```

And when a 30-day note for $750.00 bearing interest at 6 per cent is given to M. R. Richman, a creditor, the entry is:

```
M. R. Richman (an account payable) ............................... 750.00
      Notes payable .............................................................          750.00
```

The entry upon payment of the note is:

```
Notes payable ................................................................. 750.00
Interest expense ..............................................................   3.75
      Cash ........................................................................          753.75
```

USE OF DRAFTS A *draft,* or *bill of exchange,* is a written order of a creditor directing a debtor to pay a specified sum of money. The creditor may request either that the money be paid to him or to another person or firm.

It has been shown that there are two parties to a note transaction: the maker and the payee. In a draft transaction there are three parties: (1) the *drawer* who creates the instrument, (2) the *drawee* upon whom the instrument is drawn and who is to pay the sum indicated, and (3) the *payee* who is to be paid. The drawer and the payee are the same person when the drawer requests payment to himself.

When a draft is payable as soon as it is presented to or seen by the drawee it is called a *sight draft.* And when a draft is payable at a certain future time it is known as a *time draft.*

There are two kinds of time drafts: (1) those payable at a certain time after they have been seen or *sighted* by the drawee, and (2) those payable at a certain time after the date they are drawn.

When a time draft is presented to the drawee he is required to *accept* it in order to make it effective. Acceptance is usually performed by writing the word "accepted" across the face, followed by the date and the drawee's signature. When accepted, the instrument is called an *acceptance* and has all the attributes of a promissory note. When accepting, the drawee may state where the draft shall be pay-

62

able; for example, at his bank or at his office. If not stated, the draft will be payable at his office.

Drafts are commonly used by creditors to collect past due accounts. Advance notification of intention to draw is usually given. Such collection procedure is likely to be successful if the drawee is solvent since failure to pay a draft under such conditions would have an unfavorable effect on the debtor's financial standing.

Drafts are also employed in the case of shipments by freight when collection is to be made on delivery (C.O.D.). This procedure is used if the customer's credit is limited. A sight draft is drawn on the customer for the amount to be collected and an order bill-of-lading attached.

To ship goods by freight it is necessary to prepare a bill-of-lading. There are two types: (1) the *straight bill-of-lading* which is not negotiable and (2) the *order bill-of-lading* which is negotiable. Because negotiability is required, when a bill-of-lading is to be attached to a draft the order bill-of-lading is used.

The shipper sends the draft with order bill-of-lading attached to his bank for collection. The bank sends the documents, after endorsement, to its correspondent bank in the city where the buyer is located. Upon receipt, the correspondent bank notifies the buyer; and when he pays the draft the bank turns over to him the order bill-of-lading, properly endorsed, thus enabling him to obtain the merchandise. This procedure is called *shipping by shipper's order.*

A third common type of draft is the ordinary bank check. The depositor is the drawer, the bank the drawee, and the payee is the person or firm to whom the check is payable.

When a sight draft is drawn on a customer for a sum owing, the drawer makes no entry in his books of account. He, however, keeps a memorandum record of the draft which he gives to his bank for collection. If the draft is paid, or honored, the drawer will receive notification to this effect from his bank and he will then credit the account of the drawee.

ACCOUNTING FOR DRAFTS

In the case of a shipment made by freight C.O.D., sight draft, bill-of-lading attached, the sale will be recorded with the debit to an account receivable entitled C.O.D. When the seller's bank notifies him that the draft has been collected he credits the account C.O.D. by means of an entry in the cash receipts book.

When a time draft is drawn no entry is made until the draft is ac-

63

cepted since the draft has no legal status before acceptance. After acceptance it becomes in effect a promissory note and is so treated in the accounting records.

Thus a sales transaction involving a draft resolves itself into a transaction either on the cash, open account, or note basis.

TRADE ACCEP-
TANCES

A *trade acceptance* is a form of draft that arises out of a specific sales transaction. It is drawn by the seller on the purchaser and upon acceptance the drawer has the trade acceptance of the drawee. It is then treated in the manner of a note receivable.

A characteristic of the trade acceptance is that it bears on its face a statement to the effect that the purchase of goods by the acceptor from the drawer has given rise to the instrument.

DISCOUNTING
ONE'S OWN
NOTE

When a borrower from a bank gives a note as evidence of the loan, the bank computes the interest on the loan and credits the borrower's account (an account payable of the bank) with the face of the note minus the interest. Interest thus paid in advance is called *discount* and the amount credited to the client's account is known as the *proceeds* of the note.

The bank's procedure of obtaining a note from a client, deducting the discount from the face, and crediting the client's account with the proceeds is known as *discounting a note*.

Since discount is interest paid in advance, it is treated in the accounting records in the same manner as interest paid at maturity of a note. Thus, when a 60-day note for $1,000.00 is discounted at the bank at the rate of 6 per cent per annum the entry in journal form is:

Cash	990.00	
Interest expense	10.00	
Notes payable		1,000.00

Upon payment of the note at maturity the entry is:

Notes payable	1,000.00	
Cash		1,000.00

The business, upon discounting the note, received $990.00 from its bank and at maturity the business paid the bank $1,000.00. The difference of $10.00 represents a fee paid to the bank for the service it rendered by providing funds.

The above entry for discounting one's own note would in practice be made in the cash receipts book since there is a receipt of cash. However, a problem arises as to how to show the debit to Interest Expense. A method of treating the matter is to make an entry in the cash receipts book, debiting Cash, $1,000.00, and crediting Notes Payable, $1,000.00; also an entry in the cash disbursements book debiting Interest Expense, $10.00, and crediting Cash, $10.00.

DISCOUNTING A NOTE RECEIVABLE

Not only may a business obtain funds from a bank by discounting its own note but it may obtain funds in similar manner by discounting a note (receivable) that it has received from a customer.

For example, let it be assumed that a non-interest-bearing, 60-day note for $5,000.00 is received from R. J. Koster, a customer. The entry is:

Notes receivable	5,000.00	
Accounts receivable (R. J. Koster)		5,000.00

Let it further be assumed that the note is discounted at the rate of 6 per cent per annum on the date borne by the note. The entry then is:

Cash	4,950.00	
Interest expense	50.00	
Notes receivable		5,000.00

If the note of R. J. Koster should bear interest at the rate of 6 per cent per annum there would be both interest to be received from the customer and discount to be paid to the bank. The interest from the customer is interest income and the discount deducted by the bank is interest expense. Thus the entry would be:

Cash	4,999.50	
Interest expense	50.50	
Notes receivable		5,000.00
Interest income		50.00

It should be noted that the bank computes its discount on the *maturity value* of the note—that is, the face plus the interest—because this is the amount that the bank will collect from the maker at maturity. Therefore, the discount is for 60 days on $5,050.00 at the rate of 6 per cent per annum, or $50.50.

CONTINGENT LIABILITIES

When a business has discounted a note received from a customer there exists the possibility that the note will not be paid by the maker at maturity. If the maker does not pay the note, the business will become liable to the bank for the repayment of the loan granted. Thus a business that has discounted a note has a *contingent liability* until the note has been paid. Because a contingent liability is not an actual liability, it is not recorded among the liabilities.

Other types of contingent liabilities of a business are law suits pending against the business, guarantees given, and commitments entered into that entail possible liability.

NOTES DIS-HONORED

In the event that a customer should dishonor a note at maturity the business continues to have a claim against him for the debt. However, the claim will be in the form of an account receivable.

For example, if the 30-day note of Thomas Ryan for $500.00 bearing interest at 6 per cent is not paid at maturity, the entry is:

Accounts receivable (Thomas Ryan)	502.50	
Notes receivable		500.00
Interest income		2.50

The debt to the business has grown to the extent of the interest on the note; and this interest is recorded as income.

DISCOUNTED NOTES DIS-HONORED

If a customer's note that has been discounted is dishonored, the contingent liability on the note becomes an actual liability to the bank and must be paid immediately. In fact, the bank will usually not request payment but will charge the account of the business and send notice to that effect.

The bank may take legal steps to protect its right to recover from the endorsers by having a notary prepare a Certificate of Protest, and will so notify the maker and endorsers. The fee paid to the notary for his services is charged to the client.

For example, if John Gregg dishonors a 60-day note for $1,000.00 bearing interest at 6 per cent which the business had discounted, and on which a protest fee of $5.00 was charged, the entry is:

Accounts receivable (John Gregg)	1,015.00	
Cash		1,015.00

The customer is debited with the face of the note ($1,000.00), plus the interest ($10.00), plus the protest fee ($5.00).

66

10. Other Books of Original Entry

THE ACCOUNTING procedure for cash disbursements so far outlined in this book is applicable to a small business rather than a large one. In a large business where direct supervision by the owner or owners is impractical a more elaborate system of control of disbursements is necessary. For this purpose there is employed what is known as a *voucher system*.

THE VOUCHER SYSTEM

Under a voucher system a form known as a *voucher* is prepared for every disbursement to be made by the business. Spaces are provided in this form for various kinds of data pertinent to the disbursement such as the name and address of the payee, what the payment is for, the amount, and the account or accounts to be debited. The voucher also usually contains spaces for the signatures or initials of those who are responsible for various matters in connection with the disbursement. For example, in the case of a payment for goods purchased someone may vouch for the fact that the goods were ordered on proper authority and billed by the vendor at the correct price, another may vouch for the receipt of the goods, and still another for the fact that the arithmetic of the invoice is correct. Finally, the voucher is approved for payment by the officer in charge of disbursements.

The invoice is usually attached to the voucher and sometimes some of the data mentioned above are placed on the invoice rather than on the voucher.

A separate voucher is not necessarily prepared for each invoice. If a number of purchases are made within a short period of time from a certain vendor, payment for several invoices may be included in a single voucher.

A form of voucher is illustrated on page 68. This form is merely indicative since there is no prescribed form and a business will design the voucher to suit its particular needs.

After a voucher has been prepared it is given a serial number and recorded in a book of original entry known as the *voucher register*. A form for this book is illustrated on page 69.

THE VOUCHER REGISTER

67

MILFORD CORPORATION   No. 9832

New York, N. Y. October 8, 1956

Pay to

    J. G. Simpson
    Caldwell, N. J.

Date	Description	Amount
9-7-56	Invoice No. 945	$38.60

Debit___Delivery Expense_____

Order and prices checked
    E. R. P.

Goods received
    A. K.

Invoice checked
    J. G.   Approved for payment
                                      R. J. Milford

Each entry in the voucher register consists of a credit to Accounts Payable or, as it may now be called, Vouchers Payable and a debit to one or more expense or asset accounts. A column is provided for the credit to Vouchers Payable and a number of columns for the debits to various accounts commonly debited for expenditures. To provide for debits to accounts other than those for which columns are provided a *sundry accounts* section is added at the extreme right end in which both the name of the account to be debited and the amount are inserted. At the end of each month the totals of the various columns are posted to the ledger. Obviously, the total of the *sundry accounts* column is not posted because the items in this column are posted individually.

After the vouchers have been entered in the voucher register they are usually placed in a file according to the date on which payment is

68

Voucher Register

DATE	Vou. No.	Paid Ck. No.	PAYEE	CREDIT Vouchers Payable	DEBIT					SUNDRY ACCOUNTS	
					Payrolls Payable	Rent	Supplies	Telephone and Telegraph	Misc. Expense	Amount	Account
1956 May											
1	97	345	T. J. Kennedy	500.00		500.00					
1	98	346	Payroll	1,375.00	1,375.00						
2	99		Higgins Corp.	350.82			350.82				
2	100		R. F. Henderson	150.00						150.00	Furniture and fixtures
3	101		New York Insurance Co.	53.20						53.20	Insurance
3	102		Wilson Bros.	85.00					85.00		
4	103	347	New York Telephone Co.	157.00				157.00			
4	104		Henry Richardson	146.80			146.80				

to be made. Each day the clerk in charge of the vouchers removes from the file those which are to be paid on that day and prepares a check for each. The paid vouchers are then folded, usually lengthwise, and placed in a file in numerical order. The invoice attached is folded inside.

THE CHECK
REGISTER

When a check is drawn in payment of a voucher an entry is made in the cash disbursements book or, as it may now be called, *check register*. Since the asset or expense account affected by the disbursement is debited when the voucher is recorded in the voucher register such debit is not made in the cash disbursements book. Instead, there is a uniform debit to Vouchers Payable and a credit to Cash. There may also be a credit to Purchase Discounts when such discounts are allowed and taken. Thus under a voucher system the amount columns used in the check register are reduced to three as illustrated below.

Check Register

DATE		Ck. No.	Vou. No.	PAYEE	DEBIT Vouchers Payable	CREDIT	
						Purchase Discounts	Cash
1956 May	1	342	89	King and Rogers	850.00		850.00
		343	92	Ridgeway Corporation	2,045.50	20.46	2,025.04
		344	94	William Hertz	275.00	2.75	272.25
		345	97	T. J. Kennedy	500.00		500.00
		346	98	Payroll	1,375.00		1,375.00
	4	347	103	New York Telephone Co.	157.00		157.00

The payment of a voucher is indicated in the voucher register by the insertion of the check number in the column provided. Accordingly, the total of the vouchers payable at any time may be obtained by adding the amounts not indicated as paid.

ELIMINATION OF
ACCOUNTS PAY-
ABLE LEDGER

When a voucher register is employed the accounting system may or may not include an accounts payable ledger. This is so because information regarding the amounts payable to creditors may readily be obtained by scrutinizing the voucher register or consulting the unpaid voucher file. But if it is desired to keep accounts with creditors in order to have a complete record of all business transactions with them

70

an accounts payable ledger may be maintained. In such case each entry in the voucher register is posted to the credit of an account payable and each disbursement is posted to the debit of such account.

Because of the great saving effected in taking advantage of cash discounts a business in good financial condition always pays bills within the allotted time. For this reason, when it is the rule of the business always to take discounts, these may be deducted from the amounts of the invoices when the vouchers are prepared. Accordingly, a *purchase discounts* column may be inserted in the voucher register in which the purchase discounts taken are recorded. The total of this column is credited to Purchase Discounts at the end of each month. It is then unnecessary to have a column for purchase discounts in the cash disbursements book.

PURCHASE DISCOUNTS

In a business where note transactions do not occur frequently the receipt of a note from a customer or the issue of a note to a creditor is recorded in the journal. But in a type of business in which such transactions are common, special books of original entry are used to record them. These are known as the *notes receivable register* and the *notes payable register*.

THE NOTES RECEIVABLE REGISTER

A form for a notes receivable register is illustrated on page 72. The entries in this book, the form of which is self-explanatory, run across two pages. The *when due* section makes it possible to see at a glance when the notes are due. The postings to the accounts in the *account* column are made from day to day, while the postings to Notes Receivable and to the Accounts Receivable control are made at the end of each month from the totals of the respective columns.

The items entered in the illustrative register are as follows:

(1) 30-day note for $500.00, dated December 8, 1956, bearing interest at 6 per cent, received from Ralph Green on December 10 in payment of his account. This note was discounted on December 10 at 6 per cent.

(2) 30-day sight draft received on December 17, 1956, drawn by William Howard, our customer, on Jacob Gold in our favor for $685.29. Gold accepted the draft on December 13, payable at the Manufacturers Bank.

(3) One-month note of John Harris for $250.00, dated December 20, 1956, bearing interest at 5 per cent, payable at his office, in favor of Robert Field, endorsed to our order by Robert Field, and received by us on December 22.

Notes Receivable Register

[Left page]

DATE		DEBIT Notes Receivable	ACCOUNT	CREDIT Accounts Receivable	TIME				WHEN DUE												
Received	Issued or Accepted				Mo.	Da.	Int.	Year	J	F	M	A	M	J	J	A	S	O	N	D
1956 Dec. 10	1956 Dec. 8	500.00	Ralph Green	500.00		30	6%	1956	7											
17	13	685.29	William Howard	685.29		30st.	-		12											
22	20	250.00	Robert Field	250.00	1		5%		20											

[Right page]

MAKER OR DRAWER	PAYEE	DRAWEE	ENDORSER	WHERE PAYABLE	REMARKS
Ralph Green	Ourselves			City National Bank	Discounted 12/10 at 6%
William Howard	Ourselves	Jacob Gold		Manufacturers Bank	
John Harris	Robert Field		Robert Field	Harris's office	

Notes Payable Register

DATE		ACCOUNT	DEBIT Accounts Payable	CREDIT Notes Payable	TIME				WHEN DUE											
Issued	Accepted				Mo.	Da.	Int.	Year	J	F	M	A	M	J	J	A	S	O	N	D
1956 Dec. 15	1956	R. J. Leeds	1,245.00	1,245.00		30	6%	1956	14											
19	Dec. 22	Fred Rogers	500.00	500.00		30st.			21											

MAKER OR DRAWER	PAYEE	WHERE PAYABLE	REMARKS
Ourselves	R. J. Leeds	Our office	
Fred Rogers	George Land	First National Bank	

THE NOTES
PAYABLE
REGISTER

A form for a notes payable register is illustrated on page 73. This form is similar to that of the notes receivable register shown on page 72. As in the case of the notes receivable register, the postings to the accounts listed in the *account* column are made from day to day, while the postings to Notes Payable and to the Accounts Payable control are made at the end of each month from the totals of the respective columns.

The items entered in the illustrative register are:

(1) 30-day note for $1,245.00 bearing interest at 6 per cent issued to R. J. Leeds on December 15, 1956 in payment of account due him.

(2) 30-day sight draft for $500.00 drawn on us by Fred Rogers on December 19, 1956 in favor of George Land and accepted by us on December 22, payable at the First National Bank.

THE PAYROLL
BOOK

Because a business must have available information with respect to the earnings of its employees and deductions from these earnings, as required by law, adequate records need to be maintained. The central feature of such record-keeping is the *payroll book*. A form for a simple payroll book is shown below.

The payroll book may or may not be used as a book of original entry. When used as a book of original entry, the totals of the various amount columns are posted, as shown by the posting references in the illustration. The payroll book, however, may be used merely as a memorandum book. In such case the entry for the payroll is made in the journal.

Payroll Book

Payroll for June 11-15, 1956

EMPLOYEES	DEBIT Salaries	CREDIT		
		Fed.Inc.Tax Withholdings Payable	F.I.C.A. Tax Payable	Payrolls Payable
William Green	80.00	7.30	1.60	71.10
John Ryan	75.00	6.60	1.50	66.90
Carolyn Rogers	72.00	10.50	1.44	60.06
Rose Adams	67.50	7.40	1.35	58.75
	907.40	85.50	17.45	804.45
	(162)	(87)	(88)	(90)

II.

ADJUSTING AND SUMMARIZING THE ACCOUNTS

11. Property and Equipment

THE RELATIVELY permanent property and equipment, or fixed assets, are acquired and employed by a business for the purpose of carrying on its activities. They consist of such things as, for example, a building in which to transact business, various kinds of desks, tables, chairs, showcases, machinery, and other equipment; also, perhaps, trucks to make deliveries to customers. Since these assets are used up in the process of operating the business, their cost is one of the regular expenses and must be so recorded. An exception is land, which usually is not used up.

The cost of an item of property and equipment consists not only of the purchase price but also all other costs in connection with obtaining the asset ready for use. It will, therefore, include all transportation and installation costs. These are debited to the asset account along with the purchase price.

The fixed assets are usually employed over a considerable period of time. A building might be used for thirty, forty, fifty years, or more; furniture might be usable over a period of ten years; trucks might last four or five years. Therefore, it would not be reasonable to include in the expenses of a certain period the cost of the property and equipment purchased during that period. It is more logical to apportion a part of the cost of such fixed assets to each of the periods in which they are employed.

The allocation of a portion of the cost of the various kinds of fixed assets as an expense in the periods in which they are used in the business, and thus producing income, presents a problem to which accountants for many years have given considerable attention. Obviously, it is not possible to determine precisely, in terms of money, to what extent an asset has physically deteriorated during each period.

The way the matter is treated is to make the apportionment of the cost of the fixed assets to successive periods on some reasonable basis. The basis commonly used is that of the estimated useful life of the asset, that is, the number of periods—usually years—that the asset will be used by the business for the purpose of earning income,

77

and to consider a portion of the cost of the asset an expense of each such period.

For example, if a machine should be purchased for $500.00 and it is estimated that it will be used for ten years, then $\frac{1}{10}$ of the cost, or $50.00, will be considered an expense of each of the ten successive years.

DEPRECIATION   The accounting technique of apportioning the cost of fixed assets as a part of the expense of each period is called *depreciation*. The percentage of the cost apportioned to each period is known as the *rate of depreciation*. In the above example in which the estimated life of the asset is ten years and, therefore, $\frac{1}{10}$ of the cost of the asset is considered an expense of each period, the rate of depreciation is that of 10 per cent per annum.

At the end of each accounting period the accountant makes an entry in the books for the depreciation applicable to that period for each kind of depreciable fixed asset. The entry, which is made in the journal, consists of a debit to an expense account for the depreciation of the particular asset, and a credit to an account that records how much of the cost of the asset has been apportioned against income, or *written off*.

In the case of the machine mentioned above, at the end of an accounting period of one year, assuming the machine was owned at the beginning of the year, the accountant would record the depreciation by the journal entry:

Depreciation of machinery.. 50.00
    Allowance for depreciation of machinery 50.00

The credit is made to this Allowance for Depreciation of Machinery account instead of to the asset account in order that the debit balance in the asset account will always show the cost of the asset. The allowance for depreciation account will then show what portion of that cost has been apportioned as an expense. The difference between the balance of the asset account and the balance of its allowance for depreciation account is that part of the cost which is to be apportioned as an expense in the future.

In the above example, the ledger will at the end of the first year show that the machinery had cost $500.00, that of this cost $50.00 had been apportioned as an expense and deducted from income, and that the difference of $450.00 is to be apportioned against future

78

income. If the machine had been acquired at some time during the year, the amount of the entry would be in proportion to the time the machine had been in use. If it had been used for half a year the entry would be for $25.00.

In times past, the allowance for depreciation account was called the *reserve for depreciation*. This title has in recent times been superseded by *allowance for depreciation*.

From the foregoing it is evident that the accounting depreciation of property and equipment for a certain period represents a portion of the cost of the asset that has been deducted from income as an expense. It is an estimate of the fair and reasonable portion of the cost applicable to the period.

There is not necessarily any close correspondence between the accounting depreciation and the physical depreciation or deterioration of the assets. It is an ideal to have the accounting depreciation coincide with the physical depreciation and every effort is made toward this ideal. But as it is not humanly possible to foretell exactly the length of the useful life of an asset, all that is expected of accounting depreciation is that it may be fairly in line with physical depreciation and that, therefore, the deduction from income for depreciation is reasonable.

Sometimes an asset may still render useful service after it has been fully depreciated in the accounting records. This fact does not disturb the accountant because he does not expect the accounting and physical depreciation to coincide.

ACCOUNTING DEPRECIATION AND PHYSICAL DEPRECIATION

The amount of the depreciation expense affects the amount of the net income of a business. Therefore, since it would be possible to reduce income taxes by increasing the depreciation and thus reducing the net income, the Bureau of Internal Revenue in its *Bulletin F* gives information on the probable useful life of hundreds of items. These figures have set a standard for use in computing depreciation when making income tax returns. The rates are not arbitrary but based on sound business experience through the years. It is not mandatory, however, that the accountants use the same figures in the books as on the income tax returns. But because it is desirable, as far as possible, to have the accounting records coincide with the income tax return, these standard rates are those generally used by accountants in the performance of their work.

STANDARD RATES OF DEPRECIATION

79

"DEPRECIATION"
A MISNOMER

As used in accounting the word *depreciation* is a misnomer. The word that would more correctly express what the accountant does is *amortization:* the extinguishment of the record, as the asset is used up. Depreciation signifies decline in value. The accountant, however, when performing the function under discussion is not concerned with the present worth of a fixed asset but with the apportionment of the cost of that asset as a deduction from income. Since the word *depreciation* has been the accepted term used to describe this function for many years, it is difficult to make a change in terminology.

DEPRECIATION
ENTRY AN
"ADJUSTING
ENTRY"

The periodic entry for depreciation is one of what are known as the *adjusting entries*. Such entries are necessary in order to complete the record as of the date on which the net income is to be determined. Accordingly, if the net income for a particular year is to be computed as of December 31 of that year, entries for the depreciation of the fixed assets up to that date must be made. Other adjusting entries will be discussed in the following chapters.

DISPOSITION OF
FIXED ASSETS

There are four ways in which fixed assets are usually disposed of: (1) they may be fully depreciated in the accounting records and later discarded; (2) they may be sold either before or after being fully depreciated; (3) they may be accidentally destroyed; and (4) they may be "traded in" for similar assets. The accounting under each of these conditions will now be discussed.

FIXED ASSETS
FULLY DEPRE-
CIATED AND
LATER DIS-
CARDED

When a fixed asset has been used by a business for the full extent of its estimated useful life, the credit in the depreciation allowance for that asset will be equal to the debit for it in the asset account. The accountant has then performed the function of apportioning the cost of the asset to income; and the asset is said to be *fully depreciated*.

In most businesses the debit for the cost of the asset in the account with the asset and the credit for the depreciation in the allowance for depreciation for that asset are allowed to remain in the books until the asset is disposed of. When discarded, using the illustrative case above, the entry will be:

```
Allowance for depreciation of machinery.......................... 500.00
        Machinery ....................................................................         500.00
        To record machinery discarded.
```

This entry eliminates the asset from the books.

80

In some businesses the above entry is made as soon as the asset is fully depreciated. However, although the asset will have been written off the books, a record of its existence will usually be kept, perhaps in a card file.

When an asset is sold after it has been fully depreciated the amount received constitutes a profit on the sale. The entry for the sale of the machine in the above case for $25.00 would be:

```
Cash ...................................................................................... 25.00
       Profit on sale of fixed assets.....................................           25.00
   To record sale of machinery.
```

The account Profit on Sale of Fixed Assets is a form of income account.

A fixed asset may be sold before it has been fully depreciated. When this occurs, a series of three entries will usually be required. First, an entry is made to record the depreciation of the asset from the date depreciation was last recorded to the date of the sale of the asset. Second, the total accumulated depreciation of the asset in its depreciation allowance is closed into the asset account in the same manner as when an asset has been fully depreciated.

After making this second entry the balance in the asset account representing the unamortized portion of the cost of the asset is called its *book value*. This book value obviously does not necessarily coincide with the *market value* or price at which the asset is sold, and usually it does not.

Third, an entry is made for the sale of the asset. This consists of a debit to Cash; a credit to the asset account for its book value; and, if the sales price is less than the book value, a debit to Loss on Sale of Fixed Assets for the difference, or, if the sales price is more than the book value, a credit to Profit on Sale of Fixed Assets.

For example, if a motor truck purchased on July 1, 1954, for $2,-000.00 and depreciated at the rate of 25 per cent per annum is sold on March 31, 1956 for $1,175.00, the entries in connection with the sale, depreciation to December 31, 1955 being $750.00, are:

```
Depreciation of motor trucks ......................................... 125.00
       Allowance for depreciation of motor trucks........           125.00
   To record depreciation to March 31, 1956.

Allowance for depreciation of motor trucks ................ 875.00
       Motor trucks..........................................................           875.00
   To close depreciation allowance for truck sold.
```

Cash 1,175.00
    Motor trucks 1,125.00
    Profit on sale of fixed assets................................ 50.00
To record sale of motor truck.

DESTRUCTION OF A FIXED ASSET

When a fixed asset is destroyed by accident or otherwise it is necessary to record the depreciation to the date of destruction and then to close the total depreciation into the asset account, as in the case of an asset sold. These entries will be followed by one in which an account for the loss is debited with the book value of the asset and the asset account is credited.

To illustrate, if a machine that was purchased on October 1, 1949, for $1,200.00 and depreciated at the rate of 10 per cent per annum was destroyed on January 31, 1956, the entries, since the total depreciation to December 31, 1955 was $750.00, would be:

Depreciation of machinery 10.00
    Allowance for depreciation of machinery.............. 10.00
To record depreciation to January 31, 1956.

Allowance for depreciation of machinery........................ 760.00
    Machinery 760.00
To close allowance for depreciation of machine destroyed.

Loss on machinery destroyed 440.00
    Machinery 440.00
To record destruction of machine.

If the machine was insured, any compensation received from the insurance company would be credited to the account Loss on Machinery Destroyed. Assuming that in the above case the insurance company paid compensation amounting to $400.00, the entry would be:

Cash 400.00
    Loss on machinery destroyed 400.00
To record payment of compensation by the insurance company.

The balance of $40.00 would be the portion of the loss to be borne by the business.

FIXED ASSET TRADED IN

When an asset is traded in for a new one, a gain or loss may result. However, since for income tax purposes no profit or loss should be taken on an exchange, the cost of the new asset for accounting purposes will be the book value of the asset traded in, plus whatever payment is required.

For example, if a motor truck that cost $2,500.00 and has been depreciated $800.00 is traded in for a new-model truck listed at $3,-000.00, with a trade-in allowance of $1,800.00, the entry is:

Motor trucks	2,900.00	
Allowance for depreciation of motor trucks	800.00	
Motor trucks		2,500.00
Cash		1,200.00
To record purchase of new motor truck with trade-in of old one.		

This entry shows the cost of the new truck to be $2,900.00, which is the sum of the book value of the old truck, $1,700.00 ($2,500.00 – $800.00), plus the payment of $1,200.00.

In the matter of apportioning the cost of fixed assets as deductions from income, it is not possible, as stated above, to determine precisely, in terms of money, to what extent an asset has physically deteriorated during each period. Therefore, the procedure of apportioning the cost on some reasonable basis has been adopted. It is a conventional procedure, agreed to by accountants for want of a more precise procedure.

The depreciation method illustrated in this chapter is known as the *straight-line method;* it apportions the same percentage of cost of an asset to each successive period. Another method in use in connection with such assets as machinery is that of computing depreciation in proportion to the number of hours the machines have been in operation during a period. This is known as the *machine-hour method.* The rate used is obtained by estimating a certain number of dollars of cost per hour. Being based merely on an estimate, this method also lacks precision.

For reasons similar to those with respect to depreciation, most of the rules of accounting are conventions, as will be seen from later chapters. In fact, you have already seen that the very technique of debit and credit is conventional. Accountants might reverse the entire system so that asset accounts would increase on the credit side and decrease on the debit side, while liability and capital accounts would increase on the debit side and decrease on the credit side.

The application of depreciation procedure requires judgment, not only with respect to the method to be used but also the rate. Although rates have been standardized to a considerable extent by *Bulletin F*

DEPRECIATION PROCEDURE A CONVENTION

DEPRECIATION REQUIRES JUDGMENT

of the Bureau of Internal Revenue, the information there given is rather a guide for determining the correct rate. The final decision in a particular case must be based on the facts in that case and experience with the property under consideration. Such decision requires the use of judgment on the part of the accountant aided by the judgment of others such as, for example, engineers who have specialized knowledge of the problems requiring consideration.

12. Bad Debts

PRACTICALLY every business that extends credit to its customers finds that there are usually in every period certain accounts receivable that it cannot collect. This may not necessarily be because of dishonesty on the part of its customers but because of the vicissitudes of life; businessmen sometimes fail in business and are unable to meet their obligations. The loss on uncollectible accounts receivable, or *bad debts* as they are usually called, is, therefore, regarded as one of the regular expenses of the business.

There has developed in accounting a principle to the effect that the accountant should provide for all foreseeable costs and losses when they can reasonably be allocated to the current period instead of waiting for them actually to occur. The businessman knows that he is going to have some loss on bad debts; and because by experience he can make a reasonable estimate of the loss that is going to occur on the current receivables, such estimate is made at the end of the accounting period and entered as an expense although no specific accounts have as yet been ascertained as uncollectible.

This procedure in anticipation of the loss on bad debts places that loss—on an estimated basis—in the period in which the sales to the accounts that have gone bad were made, rather than in the period in which the loss is realized. The deduction from the sales income figure adjusts it to show the anticipated realized income.

The estimate of bad debts is made on the basis of experience which is modified by an opinion of present and future business conditions. Having made the estimate, which is commonly expressed as a percentage of the total accounts receivable open at the end of the period, an entry is made in the journal in which the debit is to an expense account entitled Bad Debts and the credit to an account entitled Allowance for Bad Debts.

Thus, if the accounts receivable of a certain business should amount to $29,654.89 and it is estimated that the loss on bad debts

85

will be 1 per cent of the accounts receivable, the entry will be:

```
Bad debts ........................................................................ 296.55
    Allowance for bad debts.......................................        296.55
    To provide for bad debts.
```

This procedure is similar to that used in recording the depreciation of fixed assets. It is a second type of adjusting entry.

PROCEDURE
WHEN BAD
DEBTS LOSSES
ARE REALIZED

When it has been decided that a certain account receivable is bad and will not be collected, it is necessary to eliminate this account from the books since it no longer represents a valid asset. This is done by crediting the account receivable. The corresponding debit will be to the Allowance for Bad Debts. In this manner the allowance is gradually used up.

For example, if Peter Robinson owes $138.46 and it is decided that this account is bad, the entry to treat the matter is:

```
Allowance for bad debts.................................................... 138.46
    Peter Robinson (Accounts receivable)..................        138.46
    To write off bad account.
```

PRECISION OF
THE BAD DEBTS
ESTIMATE

The provision for bad debts is on an estimated basis and cannot be expected to coincide precisely with the actual loss on bad debts. Sometimes accounts are found to be uncollectible after the Allowance for Bad Debts has been exhausted, while at other times the actual loss on bad debts in a certain period may be less than the estimate, thus leaving a credit balance in the allowance at the end of the period. Just as in the case of depreciation of fixed assets the accountant does not expect his estimate of accounting depreciation to coincide with physical depreciation, so also he does not expect his estimate of bad debts to be realized precisely.

If accounts should become uncollectible after the Allowance for Bad Debts has been exhausted, such losses may not be debited to the allowance until a new credit balance has been created in it at the end of the period. This requires that the uncollectible accounts be left open on the books until the creation of the new allowance. If, however, it is desired to eliminate them before the end of the period, the debit corresponding to the credit in the account receivable will be to the expense account Bad Debts.

If at the end of the period there is a credit balance in the Allowance for Bad Debts, indicating that the last estimate was too high, this amount is deducted from the estimate made on a percentage basis.

It sometimes occurs that payment is received for an account receivable that has been written off as bad. This is known as a *bad debt recovery*. In such case the account will be reinstated by debiting it with the amount that was receivable. The corresponding credit will be to the Allowance for Bad Debts. The account receivable is then credited with the payment.

For example, if Peter Robinson paid his account amounting to $138.46 after it had been written off, two entries would be made:

1. To reinstate the account receivable:

Peter Robinson (Accounts receivable) 138.46
    Allowance for bad debts 138.46

2. To record the payment:

Cash 138.46
    Peter Robinson (Accounts receivable) 138.46

The procedure with respect to bad debts is a conventional one. The loss on bad debts is estimated in advance of occurrence in order to allocate this loss to the period in which the sales were made or services rendered that gave rise to the existing accounts receivable. This is in accordance with the accrual basis of accounting which aims to assign to each period the income earned and the expenses incurred, regardless of whether the income has been collected or the expenses paid for or losses experienced. In applying the bad debts procedure, it is necessary to use judgment with respect to the rate to be used in estimating the loss. Needless to say, just as in the case of depreciation, the results can only be reasonable rather than precise.

13. Income and Expenses Accrued and Deferred

IT HAS BEEN pointed out that when office supplies are purchased an asset comes into the business. But since this type of asset is used up rapidly and thus its cost becomes an expense in a short time, it is convenient to record the cost of the office supplies as an expense as soon as they are purchased rather than to record the receipt of an asset and then later to record the conversion of its cost into an expense.

At the close of an accounting period, however, it may be that some of the office supplies remain on hand unused. The cost of such office supplies is, obviously, not an expense of that period; rather it is an expense of the period in which they will be used. And just as the office supplies themselves are carried into the next period, so their cost should also be allocated to that period. In the language of accounting, their cost is *deferred* and the amount deferred in a particular case is called a *deferred* or *prepaid expense,* since they represent expenses paid in advance.

Expenses other than office supplies are sometimes paid in advance and have to be deferred at the end of an accounting period. Examples of such expenses are insurance and rent. For all such items the accountant makes an adjusting entry in order to defer the portion of the cost that is to be carried into the next period. This is the third type of adjusting entry we have considered.

Such adjustments require that the expense accounts affected be credited, since these expenses are to be reduced by the portion to be deferred.

The amounts deferred are assets. The office supplies on hand are tangible property and thus assets. When insurance premiums have not yet expired the business has a claim against the insurance company for certain insurance protection. When rent has been paid in advance the business has a claim against the landlord for use of certain premises. Therefore, when the various expense accounts are credited for the amounts to be deferred, an asset account is debited. The name of this asset account is Prepaid Expenses.

88

If, for example, at the end of an accounting period there are office supplies on hand that cost $235.00, the unexpired insurance premiums amount to $75.00, and one month's rent amounting to $100.00 has been paid in advance, the adjusting entry is:

Prepaid expenses	410.00	
Office supplies		235.00
Insurance		75.00
Rent		100.00

Some accountants place the account Prepaid Expenses in the ledger with the current assets while others place it after the fixed assets.

ACCRUED EXPENSES

At the time of closing the books various expenses applicable to the period may not have been recorded and, therefore, must be added to the record of expenses in order to determine the net income for the period.

To illustrate: in a certain business it is the practice to pay the employees their weekly wages on Saturdays. Each Saturday the payroll is prepared and its total is debited to Wages and credited to Cash and accounts for the various payroll deductions. In a certain year December 31, the last day of the accounting period, fell on a Wednesday, and as of the close of business on that last day of the period the wages for December 29, 30, and 31 had not been recorded because they had not been paid. However, this expense was incurred during the year and should be included in the expenses for that year. Such expenses belonging to a period that have not been recorded are called *accrued expenses*.

Examples of other expenses that are likely to be accrued as of the end of a period are: taxes, interest, and commissions. For such expenses the accountant makes an adjusting entry in order to include them in the record of the expenses for the period. This is the fourth type of adjusting entry we have considered.

The adjustment for accrued expenses requires that the accounts with expenses of which certain amounts have accrued be debited, since these expenses are to be increased by such amounts.

The amounts accrued are liabilities: accrued wages represent sums owing to employees, accrued taxes are liabilities to the city, state, or federal government, and accrued commissions are liabilities to agents for services performed. Therefore, when the various expense accounts are debited for the amounts accrued, a liability account is credited. The name of this liability account is Accrued Expenses.

89

If, for example, at the end of an accounting period the accrued wages are $1,250.00, accrued taxes, $500.00, and accrued commissions, $75.00, the adjusting entry is:

Wages	1,250.00	
Taxes	500.00	
Commissions	75.00	
Accrued expenses		1,825.00

The liability account Accrued Expenses is a current liability account and is placed in the ledger at the end of the current liabilities.

DEFERRED INCOME

Sometimes income is received by a business before it has performed the service for which such income is paid. A notable example of this is the case of a magazine publishing house, where it is customary for subscribers to pay their subscriptions in advance. In order to compute the net income for a period it is necessary in such case to defer that portion of the income received for which the business has not rendered the service—in this case the delivery of certain magazines. Other examples of *deferred income* are: rent income and interest income. This is a fifth type of adjusting entry.

In order to defer income it is necessary to debit the income account. This reduces the amount of such income applicable to the current period.

The corresponding credit is to a liability account since the business has an obligation to render the service in the future for which it has been paid. The name of this liability account is Deferred Income.

If, for example, at the end of an accounting period the deferred income is: subscriptions, $12,570.00, rent, $200.00, and interest, $136.00, the adjusting entry is:

Subscriptions	12,570.00	
Rent income	200.00	
Interest income	136.00	
Deferred income		12,906.00

The liability account Deferred Income is placed in the ledger after the current liabilities.

ACCRUED INCOME

In some instances income has been earned but not recorded as of the last day of the accounting period. In order to complete the record of income it is necessary to include such income. For example, a contracting company may have partly completed the work on various jobs for which it has contracts. On some contracts the work is half completed, on others one third, and so forth. It is possible to estimate, on the basis of the fee stated in each contract, the sum of money earned. The total of such earnings represents the total of income earned on the contracts. Such income which has been earned but not recorded is called *accrued income*.

Another example of accrued income is that of interest on notes receivable.

In order to accrue income it is necessary to credit the income account. This increases the amount of such income applicable to the current period.

The corresponding debit is to an asset account since the business has a claim for the sum involved. The name of this asset account is Accrued Income. This is a sixth type of adjusting entry.

If at the end of an accounting period the accrued income of a certain business is: income on contracts, $20,695.00, and interest income, $85.20, the adjusting entry to be made is:

Accrued income	20,780.20	
Income on contracts		20,695.00
Interest income		85.20

The asset account Accrued Income is placed in the ledger at the end of the current assets.

In the case of an individual proprietorship or partnership the federal tax on the net income is a private matter of the owner or owners; the business as such does not pay the tax. The owner of a business may have income from sources other than the business and he, therefore, pays the tax on all his income in one return. However, a corporation differs from the other forms of organization in this respect: it must pay to the Director of Internal Revenue a tax on the difference between its income and expenses, or net income, before taking the tax into consideration. The federal income tax is, of course, an expense of the business. After deducting this expense from the net income before federal income tax, there remains the *net income for the year*.

When the amount of the corporation's federal income tax has been computed, it is entered in the journal as one of the periodic adjusting entries. This is the seventh type of our adjusting entries.

To illustrate, let it be assumed that a certain corporation's federal income tax is calculated to be $1,875.20. The entry to record this is:

```
Federal income tax ........................................................  1,875.20
        Federal income tax payable .................................          1,875.20
```

The account Federal Income Tax is an expense account. The account Federal Income Tax Payable is a liability account that records the liability for the tax to the Director of Internal Revenue. It is placed in the ledger immediately after the account Accrued Expenses.

PAYROLL TAXES

The procedure for treating the deductions from the wages of employees as required by the Federal Insurance Contributions Act has already been demonstrated. The amount of deductions required as of 1956 is 2 per cent of the *first* $4,200.00 paid to the employee during a calendar year. Any amount over $4,200.00 is *tax exempt*.

The Act also imposes on the employer a tax equivalent to that paid by the employee. This tax is an expense of the business and is debited to the expense account Payroll Taxes. The entry for this expense, which is made in the journal, is:

```
Payroll taxes ....................................................................  xxxxxxx
        Payroll taxes payable ...........................................          xxxxxxx
```

At the time the tax is paid the entry is:

```
Payroll taxes payable .....................................................  xxxxxxx
        Cash ........................................................................          xxxxxxx
```

The Federal Unemployment Tax Act imposes an unemployment compensation tax on employers of eight or more persons for one day during each of twenty weeks of the calendar year. The rate is 3 per cent of the wages paid each employee up to $3,000.00 during the calendar year.

Unemployment compensation is financed jointly by the federal government and the various states and administered by the states. All the states have their own unemployment tax laws and these vary. Although the states may raise the rate above the federal rate of 3 per cent they may not lower it. The employer credits against the 3 per cent federal tax any payments made to the state up to 90 per cent of that tax, or 2.7 per cent. As a result the rate of 2.7 per cent has been made the requirement of most states, so that the usual payment to the Director of Internal Revenue is .3 per cent. This amount is payable annually. State laws require payments at other intervals.

The entry for the unemployment compensation tax, which is made in the journal, is:

Payroll taxes xxxxxxx
    Unemployment compensation tax (federal)
        payable xxxxxxx
    Unemployment compensation tax (state)
        payable xxxxxxx

SALES TAXES

When a taxable sale is made in a state or municipality that has imposed a sales tax, the account Sales Taxes Payable is credited with the tax, the corresponding debit being to Accounts Receivable in the case of sales on credit and to Cash for cash sales. When the taxes are remitted to the state or municipality, the account Sales Taxes Payable is debited and Cash is credited.

If the tax to be remitted by the business is a certain percentage of gross sales or the total of taxes collected, whichever is greater, the business may have to pay an amount greater than that collected. This occurs particularly when some sales have been made for amounts below a taxable minimum. The amount in excess of that collected is an expense of the business and is debited to an expense account Sales Taxes.

If at the close of a certain accounting period that does not coincide with the tax period the amount of sales tax due is greater than the amount collected, an adjusting entry will be made by a debit to Sales Taxes and a credit to Accrued Expenses. This may be included in a compound entry for accrued expenses.

ACCRUALS AND DEFERRALS REQUIRE JUDGMENT

The process of accruing and deferring income and expenses requires the use of judgment on the part of the accountant. For example, just how much of the income to be obtained from a certain job has accrued during the period under review, and just how much of a certain expense, such as the cost of the material used on the job, should be allocated to that period, requires a considerable amount of judgment. The amount of income and expense assigned will be the opinion of the accountant and those specialists on the job who furnish him with information.

SUMMARY OF PERIODIC ADJUSTMENTS

You have been shown that before the net income of a business for a period can be determined it is necessary to make various adjustments of the income and expense accounts. The adjustments that have been discussed in this and previous chapters are:

(1) Depreciation. Part of the cost of the depreciable fixed assets, that is, those that are used up in the course of operating a business,

93

is debited to an expense account for Depreciation of each type of depreciable fixed asset and an Allowance for Depreciation account for each type is credited.

(2) Bad debts. An estimate is made of the amount of the receivables that will not be collected and this amount is debited to an expense account Bad Debts and credited to an Allowance for Bad Debts which constitutes a deduction from the asset Accounts Receivable. If the business has any notes receivable that it is expected will not be collected, the sum of such notes will be included in the debit to Bad Debts and the Allowance for Bad Debts will constitute a deduction from both Accounts Receivable and Notes Receivable.

(3) Prepaid expenses. These consist of expenses that have been recorded but are not applicable to the period under review and, therefore, are deducted from the expenses of that period and carried into the next period. The entry to defer such expense is:

> *Debit* Prepaid Expenses (an asset account).
> *Credit* the expense accounts affected.

(4) Accrued expenses. These consist of expenses that have been incurred in the period under review but have not been recorded. Therefore, they are added to the expenses already recorded by the entry:

> *Debit* the expense accounts affected.
> *Credit* Accrued Expenses (a liability account).

(5) Deferred income. This consists of income that has been recorded but not earned. It is, therefore, deducted from the income of the period under review and carried into the next period. The entry to defer the income is:

> *Debit* the income accounts affected.
> *Credit* Deferred Income (a liability account).

(6) Accrued income. This consists of income that has been earned during the period under review but not recorded. It is, therefore, added to the income of that period. The entry to accrue the income is:

> *Debit* Accrued Income (an asset account).
> *Credit* the income accounts affected.

(7) Recognition of tax liabilities. The adjustment of various expense accounts for taxes, such as the federal income tax, payroll taxes, and sales taxes is effected as follows:

> *Debit* the appropriate expense accounts.
> *Credit* the liability accounts representing
> the amounts due to governmental agencies.

Let us assume that in a certain business as of December 31, 1956, the debit balance in Stationery and Supplies is $2,625.00 and that the inventory of stationery and supplies on hand is $875.00.

The adjusting entry is:

Prepaid expenses 875.00
      Stationery and supplies 875.00

After posting this entry, the two accounts affected appear as follows:

Prepaid Expenses

1956								
Dec.	31			875.00				

Stationery and Supplies

1956						1956			
Jan.	1	Balance		1,350.00		Dec.	31		875.00
July	15			725.50					
Oct.	26		1,750.00	549.50					
				2,625.00					

The accounts have been adjusted to show that the stationery and supplies expense for 1956 is $1,750.00 and that the business has an asset in the form of unused stationery and supplies amounting to $875.00.

Other adjusting entries have a similar effect on the accounts.

14. Determination of Net Income

NATURE OF
NET INCOME

THE NET INCOME of a business enterprise for a certain period of time is the difference between the income, or revenue, and the expense's of that period. Consequently, the record from which the net income is computed is that of the income and expense accounts. The total of the debit balances of the expense accounts is deducted from the total of the credit balances of the income accounts. The resulting difference is the net income or net loss, depending on which is greater, the income or the expenses.

This fact may be stated in the form of an equation:

INCOME − EXPENSES = NET INCOME (OR NET LOSS)

Since the income and expense accounts are subdivisions of the Capital account, it follows that the net income or net loss, as the case may be, changes the position of the Capital account: net income increases it and a net loss decreases it.

DETERMINING
THE NET
INCOME

After the accountant has adjusted the accounts as explained in Chapter 13, he is ready to determine the net income for the period. This is done by summarizing all the income and expenses. For this purpose a summarizing account is opened in the ledger and the balances of the income and expense accounts are transferred or *closed into* this account. This summarizing account is called the Profit and Loss account.

The process of closing the balances of the income and expense accounts into the Profit and Loss account, which is effected by entries in the journal, is known as *closing the books*.

THE CLOSING
ENTRIES

Let us assume that as of June 30, 1956, the end of a fiscal year, the income and expense accounts of Arthur Hilton, after adjustment, show the following balances:

96

Income from fees	32,579.82
Rent	2,400.00
Office supplies	1,092.83
Postage	251.30
Salaries	10,850.00
Payroll taxes	542.50
Telephone and telegraph	435.81
Depreciation of furniture	528.73
Bad debts	123.00
Miscellaneous expense	973.95

Entries are made in the journal to close these balances into the Profit and Loss summarizing account. The income accounts are debited with the credit balances appearing therein, the corresponding credit being to Profit and Loss. In similar manner, the expense accounts are credited with the amount of their debit balances, the corresponding debit being to Profit and Loss.

The entries in Mr. Hilton's journal are:

78

1956					
June	30	Income from fees		32,579.82	
			Profit and loss		32,579.82
		To close income account.			
	30	Profit and loss		17,198.12	
			Rent		2,400.00
			Office supplies		1,092.83
			Postage		251.30
			Salaries		10,850.00
			Payroll taxes		542.50
			Telephone and telegraph		435.81
			Depreciation of furniture		528.73
			Bad debts		123.00
			Miscellaneous expense		973.95
		To close expense accounts.			

The closing entries are now posted. After posting, all income and expense accounts will be in balance.

For example, the account Office Supplies (assuming the purchase of office supplies shown) appears as follows:

Office Supplies

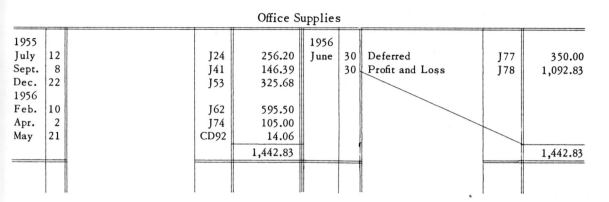

1955					1956				
July	12		J24	256.20	June	30	Deferred	J77	350.00
Sept.	8		J41	146.39		30	Profit and Loss	J78	1,092.83
Dec.	22		J53	325.68					
1956									
Feb.	10		J62	595.50					
Apr.	2		J74	105.00					
May	21		CD92	14.06					
				1,442.83					1,442.83

The adjustment, in this case the amount deferred, and the amount closed into Profit and Loss are usually so indicated in the column between the date and the posting reference.

Both sides of all income and expense accounts are now totaled and the accounts *ruled off* as shown in the illustration.

The Profit and Loss account will appear thus:

Profit and Loss

1956					1956				
June	30		J78	17,198.12	June	30	15,381.70	J78	32,579.82

The (credit) balance of the Profit and Loss account is now $15,-381.70, which is the net income for the fiscal year ended June 30, 1956.

The net income is now transferred to the account Arthur Hilton, Drawing, in order that the owner's withdrawals may be deducted therefrom. The entry is:

30	Profit and loss..		15,381.70		
	Arthur Hilton, Drawing...				15,381.70
	To transfer net income.				

After posting this entry the Profit and Loss account will be in balance and appear thus:

Profit and Loss

1956 June	30			J78	17,198.12	1956 June	30		J78	32,579.82
	30			J78	15,381.70					
					32,579.82					32,579.82

The account Arthur Hilton, Drawing, assuming that Mr. Hilton withdrew $10,500.00, will show:

Arthur Hilton, Drawing

1956 June	30			CD93	10,500.00	1956 June	30	4,881.70	J78	15,381.70

The net income of $15,381.70, less the withdrawal of $10,500.00, leaves a (credit) balance of $4,881.70. This balance, which is the portion of the net income not withdrawn, is now closed into the Capital account by the journal entry:

30	Arthur Hilton, Drawing...	4,881.70	
	Arthur Hilton, Capital...		4,881.70
	To transfer increase in capital.		

After posting this entry the account Arthur Hilton, Drawing will show:

Arthur Hilton, Drawing

1956 June	30			CD93	10,500.00	1956 June	30		J78	15,381.70
	30			J78	4,881.70					
					15,381.70					15,381.70

The account Arthur Hilton, Capital, assuming that Mr. Hilton's capital was $25,000.00 at the beginning of the period, will appear as follows:

Arthur Hilton, Capital

					1955 July	1			J23	25,000.00
					1956 June	30			J78	4,881.70
										29,881.70

Mr. Hilton's capital has been increased to the extent of $4,881.70 as a result of the income, less expenses, less Mr. Hilton's withdrawals.

Your attention is directed to the fact that the Profit and Loss account is used only to summarize the income and expenses as of the last day of the accounting period. No entries are made in this account during the period.

THE INCOME STATEMENT

After the income and expense accounts have been summarized in the Profit and Loss account, a statement is prepared giving a summary of the results of the operation of the business. This report, which the accountant presents to the management, is called the *income statement* or *profit and loss statement*. It contains a tabulation of the various forms of income and expense of the period, the difference between which is the net income or net loss. The income statement for the business of Arthur Hilton for the year ended June 30, 1956, follows:

ARTHUR HILTON
INCOME STATEMENT
FOR THE YEAR ENDED JUNE 30, 1956

INCOME:

Fees		$32,579.82

EXPENSES:

Rent	$ 2,400.00	
Office supplies	1,092.83	
Postage	251.30	
Salaries	10,850.00	
Payroll taxes	542.50	
Telephone and telegraph	435.81	
Depreciation of furniture	528.73	
Bad debts	123.00	
Miscellaneous expense	973.95	17,198.12
Net income for the year		$15,381.70

There may be appended a *disposition section* which shows the disposition of the net income. In the case of Arthur Hilton, such a section would read as follows:

DISPOSITION OF THE NET INCOME:

Withdrawn by Arthur Hilton	$10,500.00
Carried to Arthur Hilton, Capital	4,881.70
	$15,381.70

15. Illustrative Case: Adjustment and Summarization

BROWN'S DELIVERY SERVICE is owned and operated by Charles Brown. Mr. Brown makes deliveries for stores that do not have a delivery service of their own. He also acts as agent for certain stores and receives a commission on sales made for them.

Charles Brown closes his books for the year on December 31. The trial balance of his general ledger as of December 31, 1956, follows.

CHARLES BROWN
TRIAL BALANCE
DECEMBER 31, 1956

Cash	5,372.80	
Accounts receivable	7,280.92	
Allowance for bad debts		16.50
Furniture and equipment	8,740.35	
Allowance for depreciation of furniture and equipment		372.50
Motor trucks	30,850.00	
Allowance for depreciation of motor trucks		6,250.00
Accounts payable		4,092.05
Charles Brown, Capital		30,605.75
Charles Brown, Drawing	12,000.00	
Income from service charges		110,295.16
Income from commissions		3,625.50
Gasoline and oil	7,385.40	
Wages	55,253.75	
Payroll taxes	2,762.69	
Auto maintenance and repairs	5,687.24	
Rent	6,000.00	
Heat and light	884.25	
Insurance	2,850.00	
Telephone	862.74	
Supplies	6,281.70	
Miscellaneous expense	3,045.62	
	155,257.46	155,257.46

The periodic adjustments to be made are as follows:

1. Depreciation of furniture and equipment at the rate of 10 per cent per annum.

2. Depreciation of motor trucks at the rate of 25 per cent per annum.

3. The probable loss on bad debts is estimated at 1 per cent of the accounts receivable.

4. Prepaid expenses:

Insurance	$ 350.00
Supplies	872.50
	$1,222.50

5. Accrued expenses:

Wages	$853.00
Miscellaneous expense	42.65
	$895.65

6. Deferred income:

Service charges	$150.00

7. Accrued income:

Commissions	$256.80

The adjusting entries are:

		Adjusting Entries		
1956				
Dec.	31	Depreciation of furniture and equipment	874.04	
		Allowance for depreciation of furniture and equipment		874.04
		Rate 10% per annum.		
	31	Depreciation of motor trucks..	7,712.50	
		Allowance for depreciation of motor trucks....................		7,712.50
		Rate 25% per annum.		
	31	Bad debts..	56.31	
		Allowance for bad debts..		56.31
		1% of accounts receivable, $72.81, less balance of $16.50.		
	31	Prepaid expenses	1,222.50	
		Insurance		350.00
		Supplies		872.50
	31	Wages	853.00	
		Miscellaneous expenses..	42.65	
		Accrued expenses		895.65
	31	Income from service charges...	150.00	
		Deferred income...		150.00
	31	Accrued income	256.80	
		Income from commissions..		256.80

103

A trial balance of Charles Brown's general ledger after posting the adjusting entries would appear as follows.

CHARLES BROWN
TRIAL BALANCE AFTER ADJUSTING ENTRIES
DECEMBER 31, 1956

Cash	5,372.80	
Accounts receivable	7,280.92	
Allowance for bad debts		72.81
Accrued income	256.80	
Prepaid expenses	1,222.50	
Furniture and equipment	8,740.35	
Allowance for depreciation of furniture and equipment		1,246.54
Motor trucks	30,850.00	
Allowance for depreciation of motor trucks		13,962.50
Accounts payable		4,092.05
Accrued expenses		895.65
Deferred income		150.00
Charles Brown, Capital		30,605.75
Charles Brown, Drawing	12,000.00	
Income from service charges		110,145.16
Income from commissions		3,882.30
Gasoline and oil	7,385.40	
Wages	56,106.75	
Payroll taxes	2,762.69	
Auto maintenance and repairs	5,687.24	
Rent	6,000.00	
Heat and light	884.25	
Insurance	2,500.00	
Telephone	862.74	
Supplies	5,409.20	
Miscellaneous expense	3,088.27	
Depreciation of furniture and equipment	874.04	
Depreciation of motor trucks	7,712.50	
Bad debts	56.31	
	165,052.76	165,052.76

The tabulation on page 105 shows how the above account balances result from applying the adjustments to the original trial balance.

The closing entries are shown at the top of page 106.

THE
POST-CLOSING
TRIAL BALANCE

A trial balance taken from the ledger after posting the closing entries, known as a *post-closing trial balance,* is shown in the lower part of page 106.

It is customary to take off a post-closing trial balance in order to make certain that the ledger balances after the books have been closed. Note that it contains only the balances of the asset and li-

	TRIAL BALANCE		ADJUSTMENTS		TRIAL BALANCE AFTER ADJUSTMENT	
	DR.	CR.	DR.	CR.	DR.	CR.
Cash	5,372.80				5,372.80	
Accounts receivable	7,280.92				7,280.92	
Allowance for bad debts		16.50		(3) 56.31		72.81
Accrued income			(7) 256.80		256.80	
Prepaid expenses			(4) 1,222.50		1,222.50	
Furniture and equipment	8,740.35				8,740.35	
Allowance for depreciation of furniture and equipment		372.50		(1) 874.04		1,246.54
Motor trucks	30,850.00				30,850.00	
Allowance for depreciation of motor trucks		6,250.00		(2) 7,712.50		13,962.50
Accounts payable		4,092.05				4,092.05
Accrued expenses				(5) 895.65		895.65
Deferred income				(6) 150.00		150.00
Charles Brown, Capital		30,605.75				30,605.75
Charles Brown, Drawing	12,000.00				12,000.00	
Income from service charges		110,295.16	(6) 150.00			110,145.16
Income from commissions		3,625.50		(7) 256.80		3,882.30
Gasoline and oil	7,385.40				7,385.40	
Wages	55,253.75		(5) 853.00		56,106.75	
Payroll taxes	2,762.69				2,762.69	
Auto maintenance and repairs	5,687.24				5,687.24	
Rent	6,000.00				6,000.00	
Heat and light	884.25				884.25	
Insurance	2,850.00			(4) 350.00	2,500.00	
Telephone	862.74				862.74	
Supplies	6,281.70			(4) 872.50	5,409.20	
Miscellaneous expense	3,045.62		(5) 42.65		3,088.27	
Depreciation of furniture and equipment			(1) 874.04		874.04	
Depreciation of motor trucks			(2) 7,712.50		7,712.50	
Bad debts			(3) 56.31		56.31	
	155,257.46	155,257.46	11,167.80	11,167.80	165,052.76	165,052.76

		Closing Entries		
1956				
Dec.	31	Income from service charges..	110,145.16	
		Income from commissions...	3,882.30	
		Profit and loss		114,027.46
	31	Profit and loss	99,329.39	
		Gasoline and oil		7,385.40
		Wages		56,106.75
		Payroll taxes		2,762.69
		Auto maintenance and repairs		5,687.24
		Rent..		6,000.00
		Heat and light		884.25
		Insurance		2,500.00
		Telephone...		862.74
		Supplies		5,409.20
		Miscellaneous expense...		3,088.27
		Depreciation of furniture and equipment		874.04
		Depreciation of motor trucks...		7,712.50
		Bad debts		56.31
	31	Profit and loss	14,698.07	
		Charles Brown, Drawing...		14,698.07
	31	Charles Brown, Drawing...	2,698.07	
		Charles Brown, Capital		2,698.07

CHARLES BROWN
POST-CLOSING TRIAL BALANCE
DECEMBER 31, 1956

Cash	5,372.80	
Accounts receivable...	7,280.92	
Allowance for bad debts...		72.81
Accrued income	256.80	
Prepaid expenses	1,222.50	
Furniture and equipment...	8,740.35	
Allowance for depreciation of furniture and equipment		1,246.54
Motor trucks	30,850.00	
Allowance for depreciation of motor trucks............................		13,962.50
Accounts payable		4,092.05
Accrued expenses		895.65
Deferred income..		150.00
Charles Brown, Capital		33,303.82
	53,723.37	53,723.37

ability accounts and the Capital account. The tabulation on page 108 shows how the above balances result from the closing of the balances of the income and expense accounts into the Profit and Loss account and the closing of the balances of the Profit and Loss and the Drawing account into the Capital account.

The sole purpose of the adjusting entries is to make the accounting records show, at the time of closing the books, the income and expense in accordance with the accrual basis of accounting. This requires that the income earned be shown, whether collected or not, and the expenses incurred, whether paid for or not. To achieve this, certain recorded income that has not been earned and certain recorded expenses that have not been incurred must be taken out of the record of income and expense, or deferred. Also, income that has been earned but not recorded and expenses that have been incurred but not recorded must be added to the record of income and expense, or accrued.

REVERSAL OF THE ADJUSTING ENTRIES

Having achieved the desired result: the net income on the accrual basis of accounting, the four accounts created solely for the purpose of making these adjustments—Prepaid Expenses, Accrued Expenses, Deferred Income, and Accrued Income—are closed out by reversing the entries that created them. This is done as of the first day of the new period.

The four reversing entries in our illustrative case of Charles Brown are as follows:

1957		Reversing Entries			
Jan.	1	Insurance		350.00	
		Supplies		872.50	
		Prepaid expenses			1,222.50
	1	Accrued expenses		895.65	
		Wages			853.00
		Miscellaneous expense			42.65
	1	Deferred income		150.00	
		Income from service charges			150.00
	1	Income from commissions		256.80	
		Accrued income			256.80

	TRIAL BALANCE AFTER ADJUSTMENT		INCOME AND EXPENSE CLOSED INTO PROFIT AND LOSS		TRANSFERRED TO CAPITAL ACCOUNT		POST-CLOSING TRIAL BALANCE	
	DR.	CR.	DR. P & L	CR. P & L	DR.	CR.	DR.	CR.
Cash	5,372.80						5,372.80	
Accounts receivable	7,280.92						7,280.92	
Allowance for bad debts		72.81						72.81
Accrued income	256.80						256.80	
Prepaid expenses	1,222.50						1,222.50	
Furniture and equipment	8,740.35						8,740.35	
Allowance for depreciation of furniture and equipment		1,246.54						1,246.54
Motor trucks	30,850.00						30,850.00	
Allowance for depreciation of motor trucks		13,962.50						13,962.50
Accounts payable		4,092.05						4,092.05
Accrued expenses		895.65						895.65
Deferred income		150.00						150.00
Charles Brown, Capital		30,605.75				14,698.07		33,303.82
Charles Brown, Drawing	12,000.00				12,000.00	12,000.00		
Income from service charges		110,145.16		110,145.16				
Income from commissions		3,882.30		3,882.30				
Gasoline and oil	7,385.40		7,385.40					
Wages	56,106.75		56,106.75					
Payroll taxes	2,762.69		2,762.69					
Auto maintenance and repairs	5,687.24		5,687.24					
Rent	6,000.00		6,000.00					
Heat and light	884.25		884.25					
Insurance	2,500.00		2,500.00					
Telephone	862.74		862.74					
Supplies	5,409.20		5,409.20					
Miscellaneous expense	3,088.27		3,088.27					
Depreciation of furniture and equipment	874.04		874.04					
Depreciation of motor trucks	7,712.50		7,712.50					
Bad debts	56.31		56.31					
Profit and loss (Net income for the year)			14,698.07		14,698.07			
	165,052.76	165,052.76	114,027.46	114,027.46	26,698.07	26,698.07	53,723.37	53,723.37

When adjusting for prepaid expenses, that portion of the recorded expense items that has not been used up and that is, therefore, an asset of the business is transferred to the asset account Prepaid Expenses. In reversing the adjustment, the deferred items, which presumably will be used up in the new period, are returned to the expense accounts as of the first day of that period.

Deferred income, which consists of income that has been received but not earned, will presumably be earned in the new period, and so, in a manner similar to that used for the prepaid expenses, the deferred income is returned to the income accounts.

The effect of the reversal of the entries for accrued expenses and accrued income is a little more difficult to understand. When adjusting for accrued expenses, certain unrecorded expenses are added to the record, and since a liability exists for these expenses, the liability account Accrued Expenses is credited. In reversing the adjustment, the various expense accounts are credited in the new period for expenses accrued in the previous period. This credit constitutes a deduction from debits which will be made in these accounts when the expenses for which the accruals were made are recorded.

To illustrate, let us take the accrued wages in the case of Charles Brown. If we assume that as of December 31, 1956, the balance to date has been brought forward to a new page in the ledger and that the adjusting and closing entries have been posted, the Wages account will appear thus:

Wages

1956					1956			
Dec.	31	Brought forward	55,253.75		Dec.	31	Profit and loss	56,106.75
	31	Accrued	853.00					
			56,106.75					56,106.75

After posting the reversing entry and the entry for the next payroll, January 4, 1957, $1,056.80, the account will show:

Wages

1956					1956			
Dec.	31	Brought forward	55,253.75		Dec.	31	Profit and loss	56,106.75
	31	Accrued	853.00					
			56,106.75					56,106.75
1957					1957			
Jan.	4	203.80	1,056.80		Jan.	1	Accrued	853.00

109

It is obvious that the payroll of January 4, 1957, consists of two parts: a part amounting to $853.00 incurred in 1956, and a part amounting to $203.80, incurred in 1957. The result has been achieved of putting each of these parts into the expense record of the year to which it belongs, as required by the accrual basis of accounting.

When adjusting for accrued income, certain unrecorded income is added to the record, and since such accrued income is an asset, the asset account Accrued Income is debited. In reversing the adjustment, the appropriate income account is debited in the new period for the income accrued in the previous period. This debit constitutes a deduction from credits which will be made when the income for which the accrual was made is recorded.

To illustrate: let us take the accrued commissions in the case of Charles Brown. If we assume that as of December 31, 1956, the balance to date of the Income from Commissions account has been brought forward to a new page in the ledger and that the adjusting and closing entries have been posted, the account will appear thus:

Income from Commissions

1956 Dec.	31	Profit and loss		3,882.30	1956 Dec.	31	Brought forward		3,625.50
						31	Accrued		256.80
				3,882.30					3,882.30

After posting the reversing entry and the entry on January 31, 1957, for the January commissions, amounting to $562.37 that have been billed, the account will show:

Income from Commissions

1956 Dec.	31	Profit and loss		3,882.30	1956 Dec.	31	Brought forward		3,625.50
						31	Accrued		256.80
				3,882.30					3,882.30
1957 Jan.	1	Accrued		256.80	1957 Jan.	31		305.57	562.37

Note that the commissions billed in January consist of two parts: a part amounting to $256.80, earned in 1956, and a part amounting to $305.57, earned in 1957. The result has been achieved of putting each of these parts into the earnings record of the year to which it belongs, as required by the accrual basis of accounting.

110

Finally, the income and expense accounts, the Profit and Loss account, and the Drawing account having been closed out and ruled off,
the only accounts remaining open are the asset and liability accounts
and the Capital account, as can be seen from the post-closing trial
balance. The balances of these accounts are now inserted on the
lesser side and *brought down* as the opening balances of the accounts
in the next period. The account of James Adams will be taken as an
illustration.

BRINGING DOWN
THE BALANCES

James Adams

1956				1956			
Jan.	26		500.00	Feb.	28		500.00
Apr.	23		375.62	May	24		375.62
Oct.	5		732.50	Nov.	7		732.50
Dec.	14		350.00	Dec.	31	Balance	350.00
			1,958.12				1,958.12
1957							
Jan.	1	Balance	350.00				

Those accounts that are in balance are, obviously, simply ruled
off.

16. The Financial Statements

AT THE END of an accounting period, the accountant summarizes the income and expenses in a statement known as the income statement, the conclusion of which is the net income (or net loss) for the period, as explained in Chapter 14.

The income statement of Charles Brown for the year ended December 31, 1956, in Chapter 15 is shown below. This statement comprises the data contained in the *income and expense* columns of the tabulation on page 108.

CHARLES BROWN
INCOME STATEMENT
FOR THE YEAR ENDED DECEMBER 31, 1956

INCOME:

Service charges	$110,145.16	
Commissions	3,882.30	
Total income		$114,027.46

EXPENSES:

Gasoline and oil	$ 7,385.40	
Wages	56,106.75	
Payroll taxes	2,762.69	
Auto maintenance and repairs	5,687.24	
Rent	6,000.00	
Heat and light	884.25	
Insurance	2,500.00	
Telephone	862.74	
Supplies	5,409.20	
Miscellaneous expense	3,088.27	
Depreciation of furniture and equipment	874.04	
Depreciation of motor trucks	7,712.50	
Bad debts	56.31	
Total expenses		99,329.39
Net income for the year		$ 14,698.07

The data contained in the post-closing trial balance, that is, the amounts of the assets, liabilities, and capital after the books have been closed, may be arranged in the form of a statement known as the *balance sheet*. Such a statement for the business of Charles Brown as of December 31, 1956, is shown below.

CHARLES BROWN
BALANCE SHEET
DECEMBER 31, 1956

Assets

CURRENT ASSETS:

Cash		$ 5,372.80	
Accounts receivable	$ 7,280.92		
Less Allowance for bad debts	72.81	7,208.11	
Accrued income		256.80	
Prepaid expenses		1,222.50	
Total current assets			$14,060.21

FIXED ASSETS:

Furniture and equipment	$ 8,740.35		
Less Allowance for depreciation	1,246.54	$ 7,493.81	
Motor trucks	$30,850.00		
Less Allowance for depreciation	13,962.50	16,887.50	
Total fixed assets		24,381.31	
		$38,441.52	

Liabilities and Capital

CURRENT LIABILITIES:

Accounts payable	$ 4,092.05	
Accrued expenses	895.65	
Total current liabilities	$ 4,987.70	
DEFERRED INCOME	150.00	
Total liabilities	$ 5,137.70	
CHARLES BROWN, CAPITAL	33,303.82	
	$38,441.52	

It is seen that the arrangement of the items in the balance sheet is in the order in which they are found in the ledger and in the post-closing trial balance. They, however, have been classified into groups and the groups have been totaled. Also, the total of the assets has been shown and this is equal to the total of the liabilities and capital, which has also been indicated. The balance sheet thus shows that the assets are equal to the liabilities and capital, as required by the rules of accounting. And since this statement proves the equality

113

or balance of the assets with the liabilities and capital, it has been given the title it bears.

The balance sheet is the culmination of the technique of double-entry accounting procedure. This technique has three phases: (1) the *recording* of business transactions in books of original entry, (2) the *classification* of the components (debits and credits) of the entries in accounts, and (3) the *summarization* of the results.

The accounting record is a financial record for it is kept in terms of monetary units; and each account contains the financial record of an asset, a liability, the capital, or one of the subdivisions of the record of capital. The balance of each account is the *position* of the record it contains as of a certain date. Therefore, the balance sheet, because it is a summary of the balances or positions of all the accounts, is in the nature of a master account or summary of the *financial position* of the accounting. In fact, a name for the statement which has in recent years come into use is that of *position statement* or *statement of financial position*.

It has sometimes been said that the balance sheet shows the financial condition of a business. However, the use of the word "condition" is apt to be misleading because it has too broad a significance. Its use gives the impression that the balance sheet shows all aspects of the relation of an enterprise to the business world about it. But this is not so. There are many factors affecting the condition of a business that are not shown in a balance sheet; for example, contracts, commitments, technical problems in an industry, market conditions, taxation, tariffs, the public's demand for commodities, and the ability of the management. The information contained in the balance sheet is restricted to that contained in the accounts. Therefore, rather than to say that it is a statement of the financial condition of a business, it is more correct to say that it is a statement of the financial position of the accounting for that business.

The balance sheet is sometimes referred to as a *statement of assets and liabilities*, or a *statement of assets, liabilities, and capital*. Either of these titles is quite appropriate, the second being more precise; but the name *balance sheet* is in most common use.

It is held by many that the title *balance sheet* indicates that the statement has been derived from a double-entry system of accounting whereas a *statement of assets and liabilities* might be compiled from sources other than a double-entry accounting system.

114

The balance sheet and the income statement together are usually referred to as *the financial statements*. The preparation of these statements is part of the accounting procedure. They constitute a summary of the accounting at the end of a period, the balance sheet showing the status of the assets, the liabilities, and the capital, and the income statement the result of operations leading to the present status. Thus the two statements are complementary. Both contain data of great importance to those interested in the business.

The income statement of Charles Brown for the year ended December 31, 1955, is shown below.

CHARLES BROWN
INCOME STATEMENT
FOR THE YEAR ENDED DECEMBER 31, 1955

INCOME:

Service charges	$96,492.80	
Commissions	2,350.75	
Total income		$98,843.55

EXPENSES:

Gasoline and oil	$ 6,025.47	
Wages	48,392.50	
Payroll taxes	2,177.66	
Auto maintenance and repairs	4,135.09	
Rent	6,000.00	
Heat and light	923.50	
Insurance	1,975.00	
Telephone	750.25	
Supplies	4,826.90	
Miscellaneous expense	3,426.87	
Depreciation of furniture and equipment	285.50	
Depreciation of motor trucks	3,850.00	
Bad debts	24.00	
Total expenses		82,792.74
Net income for the year		$16,050.81

This income statement may be placed in juxtaposition with Brown's income statement for the year ended December 31, 1956, and the differences in the various income and expense items tabulated. A statement so arranged is called a *comparative income statement*.

Charles Brown's comparative income statement for the years ended December 31, 1955 and 1956, is on page 116. From this statement we

CHARLES BROWN
COMPARATIVE INCOME STATEMENT
FOR THE YEARS ENDED DECEMBER 31, 1955 AND 1956

	1956	1955	*Increase Decrease* *
INCOME:			
Service charges	$110,145.16	$96,492.80	$13,652.36
Commissions	3,882.30	2,350.75	1,531.55
Total income	$114,027.46	$98,843.55	$15,183.91
EXPENSES:			
Gasoline and oil	$ 7,385.40	$ 6,025.47	$ 1,359.93
Wages	56,106.75	48,392.50	7,714.25
Payroll taxes	2,762.69	2,177.66	585.03
Auto maintenance and repairs	5,687.24	4,135.09	1,552.15
Rent	6,000.00	6,000.00	–
Heat and light	884.25	923.50	39.25*
Insurance	2,500.00	1,975.00	525.00
Telephone	862.74	750.25	112.49
Supplies	5,409.20	4,826.90	582.30
Miscellaneous expense	3,088.27	3,426.87	338.60*
Depreciation of furniture and equipment	874.04	285.50	588.54
Depreciation of motor trucks	7,712.50	3,850.00	3,862.50
Bad debts	56.31	24.00	32.31
Total expenses	$ 99,329.39	$82,792.74	$16,536.65
Net income for the year	$ 14,698.07	$16,050.81	$ 1,352.74*

learn that although Mr. Brown's income during 1956 was $15,183.91 more than in 1955, his net income for 1956 was $1,352.74 less than in 1955. This decline in net income was caused by the fact that the expenses increased in 1956 in the amount of $16,536.65, which exceeds the increase in income by $1,352.74. Such information regarding the variation in net income and its causes is extremely important. This is an illustration of how the accountant aids in the management of a business by supplying vital information.

COMPARATIVE BALANCE SHEET   A *comparative balance sheet* may be prepared similar in arrangement to that of the comparative income statement. The comparative balance sheet, by comparing the position of each of the asset and liability accounts and the Capital account as of two balance-sheet dates, provides information regarding the change—either increase or decrease—in the position of the item represented by each account. This information is of great value, for a summary of the changes that have taken place in an interval of time is a useful aid in forming an opinion regarding the status of a business.

The balance sheet of Charles Brown as of December 31, 1955, is shown below. His comparative balance sheet as of December 31, 1955 and 1956, is shown on page 118. From this we learn such facts as that Mr. Brown's capital increased in the amount of $2,698.07, that additional fixed assets to the extent of $11,173.63 were acquired, and that the liabilities were increased in the amount of $2,350.65.

CHARLES BROWN
BALANCE SHEET
DECEMBER 31, 1955

Assets

CURRENT ASSETS:

Cash		$ 3,729.62	
Accounts receivable	$ 6,050.29		
Less Allowance for bad debts	24.00	6,026.29	
Prepaid expenses		1,842.67	
Total current assets			$11,598.58

FIXED ASSETS:

Furniture and equipment	$ 3,062.70		
Less Allowance for depreciation	372.50	$ 2,690.20	
Motor trucks	$25,354.02		
Less Allowance for depreciation	6,250.00	19,104.02	
Total fixed assets			21,794.22
			$33,392.80

Liabilities and Capital

CURRENT LIABILITIES:

Accounts payable	$ 1,823.32	
Accrued expenses	963.73	
Total current liabilities		$ 2,787.05
CHARLES BROWN, CAPITAL		30,605.75
		$33,392.80

117

CHARLES BROWN
COMPARATIVE BALANCE SHEET
DECEMBER 31, 1955 AND 1956

	December 31 1956	1955	Increase Decrease *
Assets			
CURRENT ASSETS:			
Cash	$ 5,372.80	$ 3,729.62	$ 1,643.18
Accounts receivable	7,280.92	6,050.29	1,230.63
Accrued income	256.80	—	256.80
Prepaid expenses	1,222.50	1,842.67	620.17*
	$14,133.02	$11,622.58	$ 2,510.44
Less Allowance for bad debts........................	72.81	24.00	48.81
Total current assets	$14,060.21	$11,598.58	$ 2,461.63
FIXED ASSETS:			
Furniture and equipment.....................................	$ 8,740.35	$ 3,062.70	$ 5,677.65
Motor trucks	30,850.00	25,354.02	5,495.98
	$39,590.35	$28,416.72	$11,173.63
Less Allowances for depreciation:			
Furniture and equipment.............................	$ 1,246.54	$ 372.50	$ 874.04
Motor trucks	13,962.50	6,250.00	7,712.50
	$15,209.04	$ 6,622.50	$ 8,586.54
Net fixed assets....................	$24,381.31	$21,794.22	$ 2,587.09
	$38,441.52	$33,392.80	$ 5,048.72
Liabilities and Capital			
CURRENT LIABILITIES:			
Accounts payable ....$	4,092.05	$ 1,823.32	$ 2,268.73
Accrued expenses	895.65	963.73	68.08*
Total current liabilities	$ 4,987.70	$ 2,787.05	$ 2,200.65
DEFERRED INCOME	150.00	—	150.00
Total liabilities....................	$ 5,137.70	$ 2,787.05	$ 2,350.65
CHARLES BROWN, CAPITAL	33,303.82	30,605.75	2,698.07
	$38,441.52	$33,392.80	$ 5,048.72

III.
MERCHANDISING

17. Accounting for a Merchandising Business

IN THE FOREGOING chapters the illustrations were limited to businesses that sell services. We shall now consider a business that sells merchandise. In a service business, as you have seen, the main source of income is the charges for the service rendered. In a merchandising enterprise it is the difference between the *cost of goods sold* and what they are sold for. INCOME OF A MERCHANDISING BUSINESS

Accounting for the income of a merchandising or trading business is more complex than accounting for the income of a service business. The income is easily ascertained in a service business for it is shown by the credit balance in the account kept for that purpose. In a trading business it is more difficult to ascertain the income because the cost of the goods sold must be determined.

If to the inventory of merchandise on hand at the beginning of a period there is added the cost of the goods purchased during the period plus the cost of freight and cartage on those goods, and then there is deducted the price of any goods that have been returned to the vendor, the remainder will be the cost of all the merchandise to be accounted for. If from this figure the inventory of goods still on hand is deducted, the difference will be the cost of the goods sold. COST OF GOODS SOLD

This is demonstrated by the following example:

Merchandise inventory, January 1	$ 8,269.40
Add purchases of merchandise	22,487.61
	$30,757.01
Add freight and cartage on purchases	269.50
	$31,026.51
Less purchases returned to vendor	385.00
Merchandise to be accounted for	$30,641.51
Less inventory, December 31	6,584.32
Cost of goods sold	$24,057.19

GROSS PROFIT AND NET INCOME

Continuing the illustration, if the sales for the year amount to $36,472.19, and the returns and allowances amount to $843.76, the income is computed in the following manner:

Sales	$36,472.19
Less returns and allowances	843.76
Net sales	$35,628.43
Less cost of goods sold	24,057.19
Income from merchandising operations	$11,571.24

This income, which is the difference between the cost and selling price of merchandise, is called the *gross margin* or *gross profit*. It corresponds to the income from fees in a service business.

After deducting the various expenses of operating the business from the gross profit, the remainder will be the net income of the business.

If in the illustration the expenses amount to $7,472.45 (consisting of rent, $1,200.00, salaries, $5,150.00, payroll taxes, $185.00, and general expenses, $937.45), the net income is determined by the computation:

Net sales	$35,628.43
Less cost of goods sold	24,057.19
Gross profit	$11,571.24
Less expenses	7,472.45
Net income	$ 4,098.79

INCOME STATEMENT OF A MERCHANDISING BUSINESS

The income statement of a merchandising business is constructed in the manner outlined in the foregoing discussion. For the illustrative case, the statement is shown on page 123. The portion of the statement from the sales to the gross profit is sometimes referred to as the *trading section*.

ACCOUNTING FOR MERCHANDISE

Merchandise is an asset, and at the beginning of an accounting period the merchandise stock on hand is represented by a debit in the asset account Merchandise Inventory. Purchases of goods increase the asset merchandise and sales of goods decrease it. But the purchase price of an article is usually on a different basis from the selling price of that article because normally the selling price includes an increase over the purchase price, which is the seller's profit on the sale. Since the purchases and sales are on different price bases, the increases and decreases in the asset merchandise are not recorded in the same account but in separate accounts.

122

Sales		$36,472.19
Less Returns and allowances		843.76
Net sales		$35,628.43
COST OF GOODS SOLD:		
Merchandise inventory, January 1	$ 8,269.40	
Purchases	22,487.61	
Freight and cartage inward	269.50	
	$31,026.51	
Less Returns and allowances	385.00	
	$30,641.51	
Less Merchandise inventory, December 31	6,584.32	
Cost of goods sold		24,057.19
Gross profit on sales		$11,571.24
EXPENSES:		
Rent	$ 1,200.00	
Salaries	5,150.00	
Payroll taxes	185.00	
General expenses	937.45	
Total expenses		7,472.45
Net income for the year		$ 4,098.79

The usual procedure in accounting for merchandise is to have accounts for:

> Merchandise Inventory
> Purchases
> Sales

As has been stated above, the account Merchandise Inventory records the merchandise on hand at the beginning of the period. Purchases of additional merchandise are debited to the account Purchases with a credit to the account of the vendor (an account payable) or to Cash, if purchased for cash. Sales of merchandise are debited to the account of the customer (an account receivable) or to Cash, if a cash sale, and credited to the account Sales.

Occasionally for some reason merchandise that has been purchased is returned to the vendor, or merchandise that has been sold is returned by a customer. In order to handle such returns the following accounts are used:

> Purchase Returns and Allowances
> Sales Returns and Allowances

When goods purchased on credit are returned to the vendor, the account (payable) with him is debited and Purchase Returns and Allowances is credited. If the transaction is on a cash basis, the debit is to the account Cash.

When a customer returns goods, the account Sales Returns and Allowances is debited and the account (receivable) with the customer is credited. If a cash refund is made, the credit will be to the Cash account.

In some instances an allowance or rebate, that is, a reduction of the original price of a purchase or sale is made. These may be treated in the same manner as returns and included in the same accounts. However, they may be recorded in separate accounts from those recording the returns, if separate statistical data on returns and on allowances is desired.

Sometimes freight or cartage is paid on incoming shipments of merchandise. For such items an account is opened bearing the title:

Freight and Cartage Inward

This account is debited with the amount of the freight and cartage. The corresponding credit is to an account (payable) with a railroad or other carrier, or to Cash, if paid immediately.

SUMMARIZING
THE COST OF
GOODS SOLD

In making the closing entries, the cost of goods sold, also called the *cost of sales,* may be obtained by the use of a summarizing account bearing the title Cost of Goods Sold. Into this account are closed the balances of the accounts that make up the cost of goods sold.

To illustrate, let it be assumed that the following are the balances of the accounts that comprise the cost of goods sold as they appear in the trial balance of R. W. Pierce as of the close of business on December 31, 1956:

Merchandise inventory	10,289.00	
Purchases	21,682.86	
Purchase returns and allowances		364.39
Freight and cartage inward	876.97	
Purchase discounts		182.50

These account balances are closed into Cost of Goods Sold by the following closing entries in the journal:

Cost of goods sold	32,848.83	
Merchandise inventory		10,289.00
Purchases		21,682.86
Freight and cartage inward		876.97
Purchase returns and allowances	364.89	
Purchase discounts	182.50	
Cost of goods sold		547.39

Cash discounts deducted by the business constitute a reduction of the cost of the purchases, while those deducted by customers reduce the income from sales.

There remains one more item to be added to the record in order to determine the cost of goods sold: the final inventory of merchandise.

Having computed the amount of the final inventory of merchandise as $23,853.46, the following entry is made in the journal:

RECORDING THE FINAL INVENTORY

Merchandise inventory	23,853.46	
Cost of goods sold		23,853.46

This entry is in the nature of an adjusting entry, since it adjusts the books to show the final inventory of merchandise. It is thus in the same category as the adjusting entries for depreciation, bad debts, and accrued and deferred income and expense.

The account Merchandise Inventory now records the amount of the asset merchandise that is on hand at the close of business on December 31, 1956. You will recall that the balance in this account representing the initial inventory, $10,289.00, was closed into Cost of Goods Sold in the closing entry above. As a result, there is a debit in the Cost of Goods Sold account for the initial inventory and a credit in this account for the final inventory.

All of the entries to determine the cost of goods sold having now been made, the Cost of Goods Sold account shows:

Cost of Goods Sold

1956					1956				
Dec.	31	8,447.98		32,848.83	Dec.	31			547.39
						31			23,853.46
									24,400.85

The balance of the Cost of Goods Sold account, which is the cost of the goods sold, is now closed into the Profit and Loss account by the closing entry:

Profit and loss	8,447.98	
Cost of goods sold		8,447.98

Not all accountants employ a Cost of Goods Sold account. Those who do not, close the items comprising the cost of goods sold directly into the Profit and Loss account.

125

Let us now assume that R. W. Pierce's trial balance as of December 31, 1956, contains the following additional income and expense items:

Sales		30,290.25
Sales returns and allowances	250.40	
Sales discounts	207.13	
Salaries	8,250.00	
Payroll taxes	412.50	
Rent	3,600.00	
Supplies	1,340.87	
Postage	85.62	
Telephone	225.75	
Depreciation of furniture and fixtures	375.00	
Bad debts	45.00	
Miscellaneous expense	1,850.25	
Rent income		500.00

These data complete the information required for the determination of the net income. The income statement of R. W. Pierce for the year ended December 31, 1956, is shown on page 127.

The rent income is derived from subletting a part of the premises. Income that is not the result of the regular operation of the business is shown in a section for *Other Income*.

When the owner of the business takes merchandise out of the stock for his personal use, such action cannot be regarded as a sale. It is in the nature of a withdrawal similar to the withdrawal of cash. The accounting entry usually made for a withdrawal of merchandise is to debit the owner's Drawing account and to credit Purchases. The assumption in this procedure is that the amount of the goods purchased for resale has been reduced.

R. W. PIERCE
INCOME STATEMENT
FOR THE YEAR ENDED DECEMBER 31, 1956

Sales				$30,290.25
Less Returns and allowances			$ 250.40	
Cash discounts			207.13	457.53
Sales, net of returns, allowances, and discounts				$29,832.72
COST OF GOODS SOLD:				
Inventory, January 1			$10,289.00	
Purchases		$21,682.86		
Freight and cartage inward		876.97		
		$22,559.83		
Less Returns and allowances	$364.89			
Cash discounts	182.50	547.39	22,012.44	
Total goods to be accounted for			$32,301.44	
Less Inventory, December 31			23,853.46	
Cost of goods sold				8,447.98
Gross profit on sales				$21,384.74
EXPENSES:				
Salaries			$ 8,250.00	
Payroll taxes			412.50	
Rent			3,600.00	
Supplies			1,340.87	
Postage			85.62	
Telephone			225.75	
Depreciation of furniture and fixtures			375.00	
Bad debts			45.00	
Miscellaneous expense			1,850.25	
Total expenses				16,184.99
				$ 5,199.75
OTHER INCOME:				
Rent				500.00
Net income for the year				$ 5,699.75

18. The Merchandise Inventory

YOU HAVE SEEN that the net income of a merchandising business cannot be determined without having available the dollar amount of the final inventory, or stock of merchandise on hand at the end of the period. There are two types of inventory procedures in use: (1) the *periodic* inventory, and (2) the *perpetual* inventory.

THE PERIODIC
INVENTORY

The periodic inventory procedure consists of making a physical count of all articles in stock at least once a year, as of the date of closing the books. At all other times during the year there is no complete information available on the amount of the stock of goods. The periodic inventory procedure is simple and relatively inexpensive. It is, therefore, the type most commonly used.

The inventory is recorded on *inventory sheets* which show the various items in stock and the number of units of each. The units are multiplied by a price to obtain the dollar amounts.

A problem arises when a change in the replacement price has taken place since certain of the items in the inventory were acquired. For example, let us assume that there are in an inventory 78 cans of tomatoes which were purchased at 15 cents a can, but the replacement market price of which at the time of taking the inventory is 20 cents. Shall the cans of tomatoes be priced at 15 or 20 cents? Further, let us assume that there are 18 cans of peas which cost 28 cents each but which can now be obtained for 23 cents each. Shall they be priced at 28 or 23 cents?

The answer to these questions is found in the generally accepted rule of accounting that the items in the inventory shall be priced at *cost or market, whichever is lower*. Therefore, the cans of tomatoes will be priced at 15 cents each and the cans of peas at 23 cents each.

If the dollar amount of the final inventory should be increased because of a rise in market prices, the result would be a lowering of the cost of goods sold and an increase in the gross profit on sales. This can readily be seen by referring to the income statement of R. W. Pierce on page 127. If the final inventory in this statement were raised

128

from $23,853.46 to $24,353.46 the cost of goods sold would be decreased from $8,447.98 to $7,947.98 and the gross profit on sales would be increased from $21,384.74 to $21,884.74, making an increase in gross profit of $500.00.

Similarly, a decrease in the dollar amount of the final inventory would cause a decrease in the gross profit on sales.

To return to the cans of tomatoes and peas, if the cans of tomatoes should be priced at 20 cents each instead of 15 cents, the gross profit would be increased $3.90. But this increase has not been realized and can be realized only by the sale of the cans. It is a principle of accounting that no recognition shall be given to such an unrealized profit.

On the other hand, when the market price declines, recognition is given to the decline. In the present illustration, the peas would be priced at 23 cents per can, instead of 28 cents, thus decreasing the gross profit by 90 cents. Recognition is thus given to a loss of 5 cents per can, although the loss has not been realized and may never be realized, for when the peas are sold at some time in the future the market may have risen.

Thus it is seen that although recognition is given in accounting practice to unrealized losses, no recognition is given to unrealized profits. This procedure does not conform entirely with logical reasoning; but accountancy defends its position by explaining that it is prompted by *conservatism,* an attitude that fears to overstate profits but is not so fearful of understating them. It is in line with the principle that all foreseeable losses should be provided for, although in the case of the merchandise inventory the principle is stretched somewhat to include losses that may or may not occur.

The application of the "cost or market, whichever is lower" rule is not always feasible in practice, particularly in a manufacturing business. However, it is the generally accepted rule where no other procedures have been adopted.

THE INVENTORY SHEET The usual method of preparing an inventory on the strict lower of cost or market price basis is to arrange the inventory sheet with three pricing columns: (1) unit cost, (2) unit market, and (3) quantity times lower of cost or market—as shown in the illustration on page 130. The total of the third column will be the inventory. Thus, the usual interpretation of the lower of cost or market rule is that each

129

Quantity	Item	Unit Cost	Unit Market	Quantity × Lower of Unit Cost or Market
78 cans	XYZ Tomatoes......................................	.15	.20	11.70
18　　''	AC Peas...	.28	.23	4.14
				$28,569.70

item in the inventory is priced on the lower basis and the inventory is the total of the resulting amounts.

THE PERPETUAL INVENTORY

Under the periodic inventory procedure it is necessary to make a physical count of the stock in order to determine the net income. Since the making of a physical count of all the stock is in most cases a time-consuming and laborious task, it is not feasible to do this more frequently than once a year. Consequently, the net income can be determined only once a year.

However, in some lines of business it is essential to have more frequent information on how matters are going. This is particularly true in a manufacturing enterprise, for in this type of business the management must constantly be supplied with current data in order to exercise proper control. In such cases a system is used whereby a record is kept of all goods coming into and going out of the stockroom. There is thus a constant or perpetual record of the merchandise in stock. Where such a perpetual inventory is available, it is possible to prepare an income statement frequently, usually at the end of each month.

In spite of the fact that when a perpetual inventory system is used there is a constant record of goods in stock, the book inventory must periodically be verified by 'a physical count because goods become lost or stolen or they deteriorate. The dollar amount of any missing goods will be treated as a loss.

The perpetual inventory records are commonly kept on cards. These have at least three sections: (1) Received, (2) Issued, and (3) Balance, as shown in the illustration on page 131.

DETERMINATION OF COST

In applying the "cost or market, whichever is lower" rule in a period of changing prices, the "cost" of a particular commodity in an

130

inventory will depend on the method used with respect to assigning the cost prices to the goods taken out of stock. As goods are issued the cost prices may be assigned beginning with the first price at which the goods were purchased. When the quantity issued equals the quantity purchased at this price, the next price is assigned, and so forth. This is called the *first-in, first-out method,* commonly referred to as FIFO.

FIRST-IN, FIRST-OUT (FIFO) METHOD

To illustrate, let us assume the following with respect to, say, commodity X:

1956
May 7 Received 100 units @ $.25
    10 Issued 60 units
    14 Received 200 units @ $.30
    23 Issued 50 units
    30 Issued 160 units

These events would be recorded on a perpetual inventory stock card in the following manner:

Date	RECEIVED			ISSUED			BALANCE		
	Units	Price	Amount	Units	Price	Amount	Units	Price	Amount
1956									
May 7	100	.25	25.00				100	.25	25.00
10				60	.25	15.00	40	.25	10.00
14	200	.30	60.00				40	.25	10.00
							200	.30	60.00
23				40	.25	10.00			
				10	.30	3.00	190	.30	57.00
30				160	.30	48.00	30	.30	9.00

The final inventory of commodity X amounts to $9.00.

By the periodic inventory procedure, since there are 30 units in stock and the last batch purchased consisted of 200 units @ $.30, the cost price of the units in stock must be $.30, or a total of $9.00.

In taking the goods out of stock, the cost may be assigned beginning with the price of the last units that went into stock. This is known as the *last-in, first-out method,* referred to as LIFO.

LAST-IN, FIRST-OUT (LIFO) METHOD

Under the last-in, first-out method, the inventory card for commodity X would show:

131

Date	RECEIVED			ISSUED			BALANCE		
	Units	Price	Amount	Units	Price	Amount	Units	Price	Amount
1956 May 7	100	.25	25.00				100	.25	25.00
10				60	.25	15.00	40	.25	10.00
14	200	.30	60.00				40	.25	10.00
							200	.30	60.00
23				50	.30	15.00	40	.25	10.00
							150	.30	45.00
30				150	.30	45.00			
				10	.25	2.50	30	.25	7.50

The final inventory of commodity X amounts to $7.50.

By the periodic inventory method, since there are 30 units in stock and the first batch purchased consisted of 100 units, the first price of $.25 applies to all of the 30 units, making a total inventory of $7.50.

Other methods of pricing goods issued from stock are in use, particularly in the field of manufacturing.

COMPARISON OF RESULTS OF THE FIFO AND LIFO METHODS

In the case of commodity X, when the first-in, first-out method is used the cost of the goods sold is $76.00 and the final inventory $9.00. When the last-in, first-out method is used the cost of goods sold is $77.50 and the final inventory $7.50.

Note that during the month of May the price rose from $.25 to $.30 per unit.

Comparing the results obtained by the first-in, first-out method with those by the last-in, first-out method, one finds that when prices are rising the first-in, first-out method results in a lower cost of goods sold and a higher final inventory; and, conversely, the last-in, first-out method produces a higher cost of goods sold and a lower final inventory. In a period of declining prices the results obtained would be the reverse.

19. Records for Purchases and Sales

IT IS TO BE expected that if a merchandising business makes sales
on account, that is, on credit, the number of sales transactions will
usually be great enough to warrant the use of a special book of original entry to record the sales. Such a book is known as a *sales book.*

There is no prescribed form for the sales book. It commonly consists of a loose-leaf binder in which are placed carbon copies of the
invoices sent to the customers. It may, however, be a book in which
the sales are entered from day to day.

In order to illustrate the principle of the sales book a simple form
is shown below. This form provides columns for the date, invoice number, name of customer, and the amount to be debited to his account in
the accounts receivable ledger. The total of the amount column is
debited to the Accounts Receivable control and credited to Sales at
the end of each month.

Sales Book

Date		Invoice No.	Customer		Account Dr.
1956					
Oct.	2	862	John Melville		872.50
	5	863	Mayfair Co.		1,562.00
	9	864	Adams and Smith		2,500.00
	10	865	Peabody Corporation		525.50
	31	1,257	Joseph Pearson		175.00
			Dr. Accounts receivable		
			Cr. Sales		27,735.85

Where a considerable number of sales are made for cash, these are
usually not entered in the sales book. The total of the sales for each
day is entered in the cash receipts book. If a cash register is used,
the cash register tape will be the basis for the entry.

The entry in the cash receipts book is made by placing the debit to
cash in the *Cash Dr.* column. The credit to Sales is placed in a *Sales*

133

Cr. column that is provided. At the end of each month the total of this column is posted to the credit of the Sales account.

SALES DIS-
COUNTS

Many merchandising businesses offer cash discounts to their customers for payment within a certain number of days. If this is done, the customers will make deductions from their remittances for the discounts. In such case the entry consists of a debit to Cash, a debit to Sales Discounts, and a credit to the customer's account (receivable). In order to record the discounts taken, a *Sales Discounts Dr.* column is inserted in the cash receipts book. The total of this column is posted at the end of each month.

A cash receipts book form with columns for *Sales Cr.* (for cash sales) and *Sales Discounts Dr.* is shown on page 135.

THE PURCHASE
BOOK

It is also to be expected that a merchandising business will have sufficient purchases of merchandise to warrant a special book of original entry for purchases. Such a book is known as a *purchase book.* As in the case of the sales book, there is no prescribed form.

A simple form for a purchase book is illustrated below. It provides columns for the date, order number, name of vendor, and the amount to be credited to his account (payable). At the end of each month the total of the amount column is debited to Purchases and credited to the Accounts Payable control.

Purchase Book

Date		Order No.	Vendor		Account Cr.
1956					
Oct.	1	68	Amtex Corporation		1,298.74
	6	69	Kramer and Johns		2,587.50
	10	70	J. T. Robinson		3,500.00
	11	71	Grimm Co.		875.25
	30	143	Greystone Corporation.......................................		1,200.75
			Dr. Purchases		
			Cr. Accounts payable...................		19,462.35

However, because of the common use of a voucher system, the most popular method of recording purchases is to dispense with a purchase book and to enter the purchases in the voucher register. For this purpose a *Purchases Dr.* column is inserted in this book.

It is not common practice for a merchandising business to purchase

134

Cash Receipts Book

DATE	ACCOUNT CR.	EXPLANATION	GENERAL LEDGER CR.	ACCOUNTS REC. LEDGER CR.	SALES CR.	SALES DISCOUNTS DR.	CASH DR.

Cash Disbursements Book

DATE	ACCOUNT DR.	EXPLANATION	GENERAL LEDGER DR.	ACCOUNTS PAY. LEDGER DR.	PURCHASES DR.	PURCHASE DISCOUNTS CR.	CASH CR.

merchandise for cash. However, if this is done a *Purchases Dr.* column is inserted in the cash disbursements book to record such payments. As in the case of cash sales, the total of the cash purchases column is posted at the end of the month.

PURCHASE DISCOUNTS

If cash discounts are taken on purchases, the record for a payment consists of a debit to a creditor's account (payable), a credit to Purchase Discounts, and a credit to Cash. In order to record the discounts taken, a *Purchase Discounts Cr.* column is inserted in the cash disbursements book. The total of this column is posted at the end of each month.

A form for a cash disbursements book, for use when a voucher system is not employed, with columns for *Purchases Dr.* (for cash purchases) and *Purchase Discounts Cr.,* is illustrated on page 135.

BOOKS FOR RETURNS AND ALLOWANCES

Books of original entry for returns and allowances on sales and purchases may be included in an accounting system if such returns and allowances occur with sufficient frequency. Each transaction recorded in the sales returns and allowances book consists of a debit to Sales Returns and Allowances and a credit to an account receivable; and each transaction recorded in the purchase returns and allowances book consists of a debit to an account payable and a credit to Purchase Returns and Allowances.

The transactions recorded in the returns and allowances books are in the nature of reversals in whole or in part of some of those contained in the sales and purchase books. Consequently, forms similar to those of the sales and purchase books are used for the returns and allowances books.

If returns and allowances are not made frequently they are entered in the journal which is available for all transactions for which there is no special book of original entry.

TRADE DISCOUNTS

It is common practice for manufacturers and wholesalers to issue catalogues in which the products sold are entered at *list prices* from which *trade discounts* are allowed. This is done for various reasons, such as, (1) to avoid the necessity of publishing new catalogues as prices change, (2) to conceal from competitors the prices at which the goods are actually sold, and (3) to make it convenient to grant larger discounts to quantity buyers.

Trade discounts may be either single or in a series or *chain.* If,

136

for example, goods listed at $500.00 are sold at a single discount of 20 per cent off, the price is $400.00. If, however, a series of discounts is quoted, each in the series must be deducted separately, the second from the remainder after deducting the first, and so on. For example, if in the above case, instead of offering a discount of 20 per cent, a series of 10 per cent and 10 per cent were given, the price would be $405.00 ($500.00 − $50.00 − $45.00).

The use of trade discounts has no effect on accounting procedure because the discount is deducted from the sales or purchase price before the entry for the transaction is made in the accounting records.

20. Illustrative Case: Merchandising Business

THE TRIAL BALANCE of the partnership of Boggs and Lee as of the close of business on December 31, 1956, is given below.

BOGGS AND LEE
TRIAL BALANCE
DECEMBER 31, 1956

Cash	$ 4,289.70	
Notes receivable	1,000.00	
Accounts receivable	18,908.20	
Merchandise inventory	37,542.65	
Furniture and fixtures	7,850.00	
Allowance for depreciation of furniture and fixtures		$ 2,457.61
Notes payable		1,500.00
Accounts payable		3,672.50
R. F. Boggs, Capital		30,000.00
A. K. Lee, Capital		29,659.50
R. F. Boggs, Drawing	6,000.00	
A. K. Lee, Drawing	6,500.00	
Sales		141,885.21
Sales returns and allowances	852.63	
Sales discounts	1,367.21	
Purchases	82,853.27	
Freight and cartage inward	148.00	
Purchase returns and allowances		265.27
Purchase discounts		1,852.25
Salaries	27,245.00	
Payroll taxes	1,205.62	
Rent	4,800.00	
Insurance	525.00	
Delivery expense	2,876.52	
Supplies	3,226.89	
Telephone and telegraph	438.50	
Miscellaneous expense	3,637.65	
Interest expense	285.50	
Rent income		260.00
	$211,552.34	$211,552.34

The periodic adjustments are:

1. Merchandise inventory, December 31, 1956, $43,974.25.
2. Depreciation of furniture and fixtures, $785.00.
3. Estimate of probable loss on bad debts, $186.48.
4. Prepaid expenses:

Insurance	$120.00
Supplies	325.50
Interest expense	2.00
	$447.50

5. Accrued expenses:

Delivery expense	$872.00
Miscellaneous expense	50.00
	$922.00

6. Deferred income:

Rent income	$ 20.00

7. Accrued income:

Interest income	$ 10.00

THE WORK SHEET

The trial balance, the adjustments, and the resulting data are tabulated on page 140 in a manner similar to the tabulations on pages 105 and 108. The arrangement now used is that employed by accountants in connection with the adjusting and closing of books and the preparation of financial statements. This form is known as the *work sheet*.

The first pair of columns contain the trial balance and the second pair the periodic adjustments. The tabulation of a trial balance after adjustment of the accounts is omitted, the adjusted data being carried directly into columns for the income statement data and the balance sheet data. The income statement section is subdivided to show those items that are summarized in the Cost of Goods Sold account and those that are summarized in the Profit and Loss account. Accountants who do not use a Cost of Goods Sold account place all income statement data in a single pair of columns.

THE FINANCIAL STATEMENTS

Having completed the work sheet, the accountant uses it as a basis for the adjusting and closing entries and for the preparation of the income statement and the balance sheet.

The income statement of the firm of Boggs and·Lee for the year ended December 31, 1956, is found on page 141. Note the classification of the expenses into *selling and administrative expenses* and

| | TRIAL BALANCE | | ADJUSTMENTS | | INCOME STATEMENT | | | | BALANCE SHEET | |
| | | | | | COST OF GOODS SOLD | | PROFIT AND LOSS | | | |
	DR.	CR.	DR.	CR.	DR.	CR.	DR.	CR.	DR.	CR.
Cash	4,289.70								4,289.70	
Notes receivable	1,000.00								1,000.00	
Accounts receivable	18,908.20								18,908.20	
Merchandise inventory	37,542.65				37,542.65					
Furniture and fixtures	7,850.00								7,850.00	
Allowance for depreciation of furniture and fixtures		2,457.61		(2) 785.00						3,242.61
Notes payable		1,500.00								1,500.00
Accounts payable		3,672.50								3,672.50
R. F. Boggs, Capital		30,000.00								30,000.00
R. F. Boggs, Drawing	6,000.00								6,000.00	
A. K. Lee, Capital		29,659.50								29,659.50
A. K. Lee, Drawing	6,500.00								6,500.00	
Sales		141,885.21						141,885.21		
Sales returns and allowances	852.63						852.63			
Sales discounts	1,367.21						1,367.21			
Purchases	82,853.27				82,853.27					
Freight and cartage inward	148.00				148.00					
Purchase returns and allowances		265.27				265.27				
Purchase discounts		1,852.25				1,852.25				
Salaries	27,245.00						27,245.00			
Payroll taxes	1,205.62						1,205.62			
Rent	4,800.00						4,800.00			
Insurance	525.00			(4) 120.00			405.00			
Delivery expense	2,876.52		(5) 872.00				3,748.52			
Supplies	3,226.89			(4) 325.50			2,901.39			
Telephone and telegraph	438.50						438.50			
Miscellaneous expense	3,637.65		(5) 50.00				3,687.65			
Interest expense	285.50			(4) 2.00			283.50			
Rent income		260.00	(6) 20.00					240.00		
	211,552.34	211,552.34								
Merchandise inventory (December 31)			(1) 43,974.25			43,974.25			43,974.25	
Cost of goods sold (Merchandise inventory, December 31)				(1) 43,974.25						
Depreciation of furniture and fixtures			(2) 785.00				785.00			
Bad debts			(3) 186.48				186.48			
Allowance for bad debts				(3) 186.48						186.48
Prepaid expenses			(4) 447.50						447.50	
Accrued expenses				(5) 922.00						922.00
Deferred income				(6) 20.00						20.00
Accrued income			(7) 10.00						10.00	
Interest income				(7) 10.00				10.00		
			46,345.23	46,345.23						
Cost of goods sold						46,091.77				
						74,452.15	74,452.15			
					120,543.92	120,543.92	122,358.65	142,135.21	88,979.65	69,203.09
Net income for the year							19,776.56			19,776.56
							142,135.21	142,135.21	88,979.65	88,979.65

BOGGS AND LEE
INCOME STATEMENT
FOR THE YEAR ENDED DECEMBER 31, 1956

Sales			$141,885.21
Less Returns and allowances	$ 852.63		
Cash discounts	1,367.21	2,219.84	
Sales, net of returns, allowances, and discounts			$139,665.37
COST OF GOODS SOLD:			
Inventory, January 1		$ 37,542.65	
Purchases	$82,853.27		
Freight and cartage inward	148.00		
	$83,001.27		
Less Returns and allowances $ 265.27			
Cash discounts 1,852.25	2,117.52	80,883.75	
Total goods to be accounted for		$118,426.40	
Less Inventory, December 31		43,974.25	
Cost of goods sold			74,452.15
Gross profit on sales			$ 65,213.22
SELLING AND ADMINISTRATIVE EXPENSES:			
Salaries		$ 27,245.00	
Payroll taxes		1,205.62	
Rent		4,800.00	
Insurance		405.00	
Delivery expense		3,748.52	
Supplies		2,901.39	
Telephone and telegraph		438.50	
Miscellaneous expense		3,687.65	
Depreciation of furniture and fixtures		785.00	
Bad debts		186.48	45,403.16
			$ 19,810.06
CHARGES TO INCOME:			
Interest expense			283.50
			$ 19,526.56
OTHER INCOME:			
Rent income		$ 240.00	
Interest income		10.00	250.00
Net income for the year			$ 19,776.56
DISPOSITION OF NET INCOME:			
Withdrawn by R. F. Boggs		$ 6,000.00	
Carried to R. F. Boggs, Capital		3,888.28	
½ of net income			$ 9,888.28
Withdrawn by A. K. Lee		$ 6,500.00	
Carried to A. K. Lee, Capital		3,388.28	
½ of net income			9,888.28
			$ 19,776.56

charges to income. Interest expense and special kinds of expenses and losses are classified as *charges to income*.

The balance sheet of the firm of Boggs and Lee as of December 31, 1956, is found on page 143. Note the arrangement of this balance sheet. This form in which the assets are placed to the left and the liabilities and capital to the right, which might be called the horizontal arrangement, is an alternative form to that previously illustrated, which might be called the vertical arrangement.

BOGGS AND LEE
BALANCE SHEET
DECEMBER 31, 1956

Assets

CURRENT ASSETS:

Cash			$ 4,289.70
Notes receivable			1,000.00
Accounts receivable		$18,908.20	
Less Allowance for bad debts		186.48	18,721.72
Merchandise inventory			43,974.25
Accrued income			10.00
Prepaid expenses			447.50
Total current assets			$68,443.17

FIXED ASSETS:

Furniture and fixtures		$ 7,850.00	
Less Allowance for depreciation		3,242.61	
Total fixed assets			4,607.39
			$73,050.56

Liabilities and Capital

CURRENT LIABILITIES:

Notes payable	$1,500.00	
Accounts payable	3,672.50	
Accrued expenses	922.00	
Total current liabilities		$ 6,094.50

DEFERRED INCOME	20.00
R. F. BOGGS, CAPITAL	33,888.28
A. K. LEE, CAPITAL	33,047.78
	$73,050.56

IV.
MANUFACTURING

21. Accounting for a Manufacturing Business

IN THE PRECEDING chapters two types of business have been discussed: the service business, which sells services, and the merchandising business, which buys merchandise and proceeds to sell it. In this chapter attention will be given to the manufacturing business that buys materials, fabricates them into finished products, and then proceeds to sell the products.

If in a manufacturing enterprise an inventory should be taken at any time it would in most cases be found that there are three distinct kinds of inventory:

(1) There would be materials in the condition in which they were purchased by the business. This inventory is known as the *materials inventory*.

(2) Except in the comparatively rare case in which the manufacturing process is completed each day, there would be a certain amount of goods in process of manufacture. The inventory of such partly finished products is called the *work in process inventory*.

(3) Then there would be the stock of the completely manufactured products ready for sale, or *finished goods inventory*.

Accordingly, instead of having one inventory account, as in the merchandising business, the ledger of a manufacturing enterprise has three accounts to record the inventories. These accounts are given the titles: (1) Materials, or Stores, (2) Work in Process, and (3) Finished Goods, or similar titles.

The cost of a manufactured product consists of three elements: (1) direct materials, (2) direct labor, and (3) manufacturing overhead.

Direct materials are those that constitute an appreciable part of the finished product; for example, the cloth used in making clothing.

Direct labor is the name given to the labor applied to the materials placed into the production process such as, in the case of the manufacture of clothing, the labor of the cutters and sewers.

MANUFACTURING INVENTORIES

COST OF A MANUFACTURED PRODUCT

147

Manufacturing overhead comprises the countless expenses in connection with the manufacturing processes that cannot be identified with the products. They include such items as the depreciation and maintenance of the building and machinery, the taxes on the property, and the electricity, water, and gas consumed in operations.

The manufacturing overhead includes the labor of such workers as foremen, repairmen, cleaners, and engineers. Their labor, known as *indirect labor,* although not applied directly to the products, nevertheless aids in production.

Also included in the manufacturing overhead are materials not identified with the products, such as the oil used to lubricate the machinery and the rags used for wiping. These are known as *indirect materials* or *supplies*.

The direct materials and direct labor are classified as *direct costs* and the manufacturing overhead items as *indirect costs*. The total of the direct materials and direct labor is often referred to as the *prime cost*.

COST OF GOODS
SOLD

The determination of the income of a service type of business is a rather simple matter since the income for the services rendered is indicated by the credit balance of an account created for this purpose. The determination of the income, or gross profit, is somewhat more difficult in a merchandising business because the cost of the goods sold is computed by the summarization of several accounts. The determination of the gross profit of a manufacturing enterprise is still more difficult because the computation of the cost of the goods sold is more complex than in a merchandising business.

A merchandising business purchases the goods to be sold in finished condition, ready for sale. The debit balance in the Purchases account shows at the end of the period the cost of the goods purchased.

A manufacturing business purchases materials and manufactures them into finished products. The computation of the cost of the goods manufactured makes the accounting for a manufacturing enterprise more complex than that for a merchandising enterprise because the balances of a considerable number of accounts are involved in this computation. This series of accounts of a manufacturing business corresponds to the single account Purchases of a merchandising business.

The cost of goods sold of a manufacturing business consists of:

148

Initial inventory of finished goods
Plus Cost of goods manufactured
Less Final inventory of finished goods

The cost of goods manufactured consists of:

Initial inventory of work in process
Plus Cost of direct material used
Cost of direct labor
Manufacturing overhead
Less Final inventory of work in process

The cost of the direct materials used consists of:

Initial inventory of materials
Plus Purchases of materials
Freight and cartage on materials
Less Returns and allowances
Cash discounts
Materials used indirectly
Final inventory of materials

In preparing the income statement of a manufacturing business it is common practice to show the cost of goods sold as a single item and to append a schedule of cost of goods sold showing the details, as outlined above. A typical schedule of cost of goods sold is shown on page 150.

There are two types of manufacturing accounting: (1) general accounting procedure, and (2) cost accounting procedure (discussed in Chapter 23).

A manufacturing business using general accounting procedure for its manufacturing accounting employs the same accounts as a merchandising business with the following differences: (1) there are three inventory accounts instead of one; (2) in place of the Purchases account of the merchandising business there is one with the title Purchases—Materials; (3) an account is required for Direct Labor; and (4) a series of accounts is used for the various kinds of expenses comprising the manufacturing overhead, including Indirect Labor and Indirect Materials, or Supplies.

The following is a typical chart of accounts for a manufacturing business using general manufacturing accounting procedure:

GENERAL
ACCOUNTING
PROCEDURE
APPLIED TO
MANUFAC-
TURING

149

SCHEDULE OF COST OF GOODS SOLD
FOR THE YEAR ENDED DECEMBER 31, 1956

Inventory of finished goods, January 1			$ 92,648.79
Inventory of work in process, January 1		$ 5,681.50	
MATERIALS:			
Inventory, January 1	$ 14,287.29		
Purchases	165,250.05		
Freight and cartage inward	1,854.90		
	$181,392.24		
Less Returns and allowances $2,150.01			
Cash discounts 1,549.20	3,699.21		
	$177,693.03		
Less Inventory, December 31	32,689.52		
Materials used		145,003.51	
DIRECT LABOR		117,560.79	
MANUFACTURING OVERHEAD:			
Supplies	$ 9,615.08		
Insurance—Factory	1,537.00		
Taxes—Factory	6,850.00		
Gas and electricity—Factory	7,489.21		
Repairs to factory building	5,805.92		
Repairs to machinery	2,359.68		
Indirect labor	52,670.97		
Payroll taxes—Factory	7,037.96		
Miscellaneous factory expense	5,775.47		
Depreciation of factory building	7,284.48		
Depreciation of machinery and equipment	11,575.08		
Total manufacturing overhead		118,000.85	
Total manufacturing costs		$386,246.65	
Less Inventory of work in process, December 31		11,891.67	
Cost of goods manufactured			374,354.98
			$467,003.77
Less Inventory of finished goods, December 31			108,365.09
Cost of goods sold			$358,638.68

CHART OF ACCOUNTS

Assets

CURRENT ASSETS:

- 111 Cash
- 113 Notes receivable
- 115 Accounts receivable
- 116 Allowance for bad debts
- 118 Materials
- 119 Work in process
- 120 Finished goods
- 130 Prepaid expenses

FIXED ASSETS:

- 151 Land
- 152 Factory building
- 153 Allowance for depreciation of factory building
- 154 Machinery and equipment
- 155 Allowance for depreciation of machinery and equipment
- 156 Motor trucks
- 157 Allowance for depreciation of motor trucks
- 158 Salesroom furniture
- 159 Allowance for depreciation of salesroom furniture
- 160 General office furniture
- 161 Allowance for depreciation of general office furniture

Liabilities

CURRENT LIABILITIES:

- 211 Notes payable
- 212 Accounts payable
- 215 Accrued expenses

LONG-TERM DEBT:

- 218 Mortgage payable

Capital

- 311 Charles Watson, Capital
- 312 Charles Watson, Drawing

SALES:

- 351 Sales
- 352 Sales returns and allowances
- 353 Sales discounts

MANUFACTURING:

Materials

- 361 Purchases—Materials
- 362 Purchase returns and allowances
- 363 Freight and cartage inward
- 364 Purchase discounts

151

MANUFACTURING (CONT'D):

Direct Labor

368   Direct labor

Manufacturing Overhead

371   Supplies
372   Insurance—Factory
373   Taxes—Factory
374   Gas and electricity
375   Depreciation of factory building
376   Repairs to factory building
377   Depreciation of machinery and equipment
378   Repairs to machinery
379   Indirect labor
380   Payroll taxes—Factory
381   Miscellaneous manufacturing expense

SELLING EXPENSES:

401   Sales office rent
402   Salesmen's salaries
403   Payroll taxes—Selling
404   Depreciation of salesroom furniture
405   Delivery expense
406   Freight outward
407   Advertising
408   Miscellaneous selling expense

GENERAL AND ADMINISTRATIVE EXPENSES:

451   General office rent
452   General office salaries
453   Payroll taxes—General
454   Depreciation of general office furniture
455   Office supplies
456   Insurance—General
457   Bad debts
458   Postage
459   Miscellaneous general expense

CHARGES TO INCOME:

501   Interest expense
502   Loss on sale of fixed assets

OTHER INCOME:

551   Interest income
552   Income from sale of waste

22. Illustrative Case: Manufacturing Business

THE TRIAL BALANCE of the general ledger of Charles Watson as of December 31, 1956, follows.

Cash	$ 8,963.27	
Notes receivable	750.00	
Accounts receivable	32,629.73	
Allowance for bad debts		$ 82.65
Materials	12,641.29	
Work in process	3,468.72	
Finished goods	84,341.05	
Land	20,500.00	
Factory building	132,475.00	
Allowance for depreciation of factory building		42,765.50
Machinery and equipment	92,675.83	
Allowance for depreciation of machinery and equipment		10,681.25
Motor trucks	7,620.00	
Allowance for depreciation of motor trucks		1,050.00
Salesroom furniture	2,529.81	
Allowance for depreciation of salesroom furniture		625.72
General office furniture	1,845.62	
Allowance for depreciation of general office furniture		396.18
Notes payable		5,000.00
Accounts payable		16,841.20
Mortgage payable		15,000.00
Charles Watson, Capital		267,081.55
Charles Watson, Drawing	12,000.00	
Sales		548,621.07
Sales returns and allowances	2,859.31	
Sales discounts	1,725.97	
Purchases—Materials	154,627.46	
Purchase returns and allowances		1,725.92
Freight and cartage inward	875.29	
Purchase discounts		426.78
Direct labor	107,895.11	
Supplies	9,261.27	
Insurance—Factory	845.00	
Taxes—Factory	5,285.00	
Gas and electricity—Factory	3,159.62	
Carried forward	$698,974.35	$910,297.82

Brought forward	$698,974.35	$910,297.82
Repairs to factory building	3,275.00	
Repairs to machinery	1,842.65	
Indirect labor	40,285.75	
Payroll taxes—Factory	4,727.23	
Miscellaneous factory expense	5,847.91	
Sales office rent	6,000.00	
Salesmen's salaries	62,500.00	
Payroll taxes—Selling	2,350.00	
Delivery expense	15,962.75	
Freight and cartage outward	875.61	
Advertising	8,726.82	
Miscellaneous selling expense	10,625.50	
General office rent	3,600.00	
General office salaries	32,925.00	
Payroll taxes—General	1,185.00	
Office supplies	7,286.53	
Insurance—General	345.00	
Postage	625.75	
Miscellaneous general expense	3,826.27	
Interest expense	245.00	
Loss on sale of fixed assets	127.50	
Interest income		36.50
Income from sale of waste		1,825.30
	$912,159.62	$912,159.62

The periodic adjustments are:

Inventories

1. Materials	$23,729.46
2. Work in process	10,648.25
3. Finished goods	75,862.74

Depreciation

4. Factory building (5%)	6,623.75
5. Machinery and equipment (10%)	9,267.58
6. Motor trucks (25%)	1,905.00
(*Debit* Delivery expense)	
7. Salesroom furniture (10%)	252.98
8. General office furniture (10%)	184.56

Bad Debts

9. Provision for bad debts	652.59

154

10. *Accrued Expenses*

Direct labor	$1,375.75
Indirect labor	456.00
Miscellaneous selling expense	750.19
Salesmen's salaries	675.00
Delivery expense	150.00
General office salaries	460.00
Interest expense	120.00
	$3,986.94

11. *Prepaid Expenses*

Insurance—Factory	275.00
Office supplies	762.87
Insurance—General	85.00
Postage	63.50
Interest expense	16.67
Miscellaneous general expense	762.50
	$1,965.54

12. *Accrued Income*

Interest income	$ 5.00

The work sheet for Mr. Charles Watson's business as of December 31, 1956, is shown on pages 156 and 157, the income statement for the year ended December 31, 1956, on page 158, the schedule of cost of goods sold for the year ended December 31, 1956, on page 159, and the balance sheet as of December 31, 1956, on page 160.

| | TRIAL BALANCE | | ADJUSTMENTS | | INCOME STATEMENT | | | | BALANCE SHEET | |
| | | | | | COST OF GOODS SOLD | | PROFIT AND LOSS | | | |
	DR.	CR.	DR.	CR.	DR.	CR.	DR.	CR.	DR.	CR.
Cash	8,963.27								8,963.27	
Notes receivable	750.00								750.00	
Accounts receivable	32,629.73								32,629.73	
Allowance for bad debts		82.65		(9) 652.59						735.24
Materials	12,641.29				12,641.29					
Work in process	3,468.72				3,468.72					
Finished goods	84,341.05				84,341.05					
Land	20,500.00								20,500.00	
Factory building	132,475.00								132,475.00	
Allowance for depreciation of factory building		42,765.50		(4) 6,623.75						49,389.25
Machinery and equipment	92,675.83								92,675.83	
Allowance for depreciation of machinery and equipment		10,681.25		(5) 9,267.58						19,948.83
Motor trucks	7,620.00								7,620.00	
Allowance for depreciation of motor trucks		1,050.00		(6) 1,905.00						2,955.00
Salesroom furniture	2,529.81								2,529.81	
Allowance for depreciation of salesroom furniture		625.72		(7) 252.98						878.70
General office furniture	1,845.62								1,845.62	
Allowance for depreciation of general office furniture		396.18		(8) 184.56						580.74
Notes payable		5,000.00								5,000.00
Accounts payable		16,841.20								16,841.20
Mortgage payable		15,000.00								15,000.00
Charles Watson, Capital		267,081.55								267,081.55
Charles Watson, Drawing	12,000.00								12,000.00	
Sales		548,621.07						548,621.07		
Sales returns and allowances	2,859.31						2,859.31			
Sales discounts	1,725.97						1,725.97			
Purchases—Materials	154,627.46				154,627.46					
Purchase returns and allowances		1,725.92				1,725.92				
Freight and cartage inward	875.29				875.29					
Purchase discounts		426.78				426.78				
Direct labor	107,895.11		(10) 1,375.75		109,270.86					
Supplies	9,261.27				9,261.27					
Insurance—Factory	845.00			(11) 275.00	570.00					
Taxes—Factory	5,285.00				5,285.00					
Gas and electricity—Factory	3,159.62				3,159.62					
Repairs to factory building	3,275.00				3,275.00					
Repairs to machinery	1,842.65				1,842.65					
Indirect labor	40,285.75		(10) 456.00		40,741.75					
Payroll taxes—Factory	4,727.23				4,727.23					
Miscellaneous factory expense	5,847.91				5,847.91					

Account	Trial Balance Dr	Trial Balance Cr	Adjustments Dr	Adjustments Cr	Cost of Goods Sold Dr	Cost of Goods Sold Cr	Income Statement Dr	Income Statement Cr	Balance Sheet Dr	Balance Sheet Cr
Sales office rent	6,000.00						6,000.00			
Salesmen's salaries	62,500.00		(10) 675.00				63,175.00			
Payroll taxes—Selling	2,350.00						2,350.00			
Delivery expense	15,962.75		(6) 1,905.00 (10) 150.00				18,017.75			
Freight and cartage outward	875.61						875.61			
Advertising	8,726.82						8,726.82			
Miscellaneous selling expense	10,625.50		(10) 750.19				11,375.69			
General office rent	3,600.00						3,600.00			
General office salaries	32,925.00		(10) 460.00				33,385.00			
Payroll taxes—General	1,185.00						1,185.00			
Office supplies	7,286.53			(11) 762.87			6,523.66			
Insurance—General	345.00			(11) 85.00			260.00			
Postage	625.75			(11) 63.50			562.25			
Miscellaneous general expense	3,826.27			(11) 762.50			3,063.77			
Interest expense	245.00		(10) 120.00	(11) 16.67			348.33			
Loss on sale of fixed assets	127.50						127.50			
Interest income		36.50		(12) 5.00				41.50		
Income from sale of waste		1,825.30						1,825.30		
	912,159.62	912,159.62								
Materials (December 31, 1956)			(1) 23,729.46			23,729.46			23,729.46	
Profit and loss (Cost of goods sold)					(1) 23,729.46					
Work in process (December 31, 1956)			(2) 10,648.25			10,648.25			10,648.25	
Profit and loss (Cost of goods sold)					(2) 10,648.25					
Finished goods (December 31, 1956)			(3) 75,862.74			75,862.74			75,862.74	
Profit and loss (Cost of goods sold)					(3) 75,862.74					
Depreciation of factory building			(4) 6,623.75		6,623.75					
Depreciation of machinery and equipment			(5) 9,267.58		9,267.58					
Depreciation of salesroom furniture			(7) 252.98				252.98			
Depreciation of general office furniture			(8) 184.56				184.56			
Bad debts			(9) 652.59				652.59			
Accrued expenses				(11) 1,965.54						1,965.54
Prepaid expenses			(12) 5.00						5.00	
Accrued income			(10) 3,986.94						3,986.94	
			135,084.39	135,084.39	455,826.43	112,393.15	165,251.79			
Cost of goods sold						343,433.28	343,433.28			
					455,826.43	455,826.43	508,685.07	550,487.87	424,200.25	382,397.45
Net income for the year							41,802.80			41,802.80
							550,487.87	550,487.87	424,200.25	424,200.25

CHARLES WATSON
INCOME STATEMENT
FOR THE YEAR ENDED DECEMBER 31, 1956

Sales		$548,621.07
Less Returns and allowances	$ 2,859.31	
Cash discounts	1,725.97	4,585.28
Sales, net of returns, allowances, and discounts		$544,035.79
COST OF GOODS SOLD (See Schedule)		343,433.28
Gross profit on sales		$200,602.51

SELLING EXPENSES:

Sales office rent	$ 6,000.00	
Salesmen's salaries	63,175.00	
Payroll taxes—Selling	2,350.00	
Depreciation of salesroom furniture	252.98	
Delivery expense	18,017.75	
Freight and cartage outward	875.61	
Advertising	8,726.82	
Miscellaneous selling expense	11,375.69	
Total selling expenses		110,773.85
		$ 89,828.66

GENERAL AND ADMINISTRATIVE EXPENSES:

General office rent	$ 3,600.00	
General office salaries	33,385.00	
Payroll taxes—General	1,185.00	
Depreciation of general office furniture	184.56	
Office supplies	6,523.66	
Insurance—General	260.00	
Bad debts	652.59	
Postage	562.25	
Miscellaneous general expense	3,063.77	
Total general and administrative expenses		49,416.83
		$ 40,411.83

CHARGES TO INCOME:

Interest expense	$ 348.33	
Loss on sale of fixed assets	127.50	
Total charges to income		475.83
		$ 39,936.00

OTHER INCOME:

Interest income	$ 41.50	
Income from sale of waste	1,825.30	
Total other income		1,866.80
Net income for the year		$ 41,802.80

CHARLES WATSON
SCHEDULE OF COST OF GOODS SOLD
For the Year Ended December 31, 1956

Inventory of finished goods, January 1.. $ 84,341.05

Inventory of work in process, January 1 .... $ 3,468.72

MATERIALS:

Inventory, January 1 ....$ 12,641.29

Purchases... 154,627.46

Freight and cartage inward 875.29

$168,144.04

Less Returns and allowances $1,725.92

Cash discounts 426.78 2,152.70

$165,991.34

Less Inventory, December 31 .... 23,729.46

Materials used 142,261.88

DIRECT LABOR 109,270.86

MANUFACTURING OVERHEAD:

Supplies .... $ 9,261.27

Insurance—Factory 570.00

Taxes—Factory 5,285.00

Gas and electricity—Factory 3,159.62

Depreciation of factory building 6,623.75

Repairs to factory building 3,275.00

Depreciation of machinery and equipment 9,267.58

Repairs to machinery 1,842.65

Indirect labor 40,741.75

Payroll taxes—Factory 4,727.23

Miscellaneous factory expense 5,847.91

Total manufacturing expenses..................... 90,601.76

Total manufacturing costs $345,603.22

Less Inventory of work in process, December 31...... 10,648.25

Cost of goods manufactured.. 334,954.97

$419,296.02

Less Inventory of finished goods, December 31 .... 75,862.74

Cost of goods sold $343,433.28

CHARLES WATSON
BALANCE SHEET
DECEMBER 31, 1956

Assets

CURRENT ASSETS:

Cash		$ 8,963.27
Notes receivable		750.00
Accounts receivable	$ 32,629.73	
Less Allowance for bad debts	735.24	31,894.49
Materials inventory		23,729.46
Work in process inventory		10,648.25
Finished goods inventory		75,862.74
Accrued income		5.00
Prepaid expenses		1,965.54
Total current assets		$153,818.75

PROPERTY, PLANT, AND EQUIPMENT:

Land		$20,500.00
Factory building	$132,475.00	
Less Allowance for depreciation	49,389.25	83,085.75
Machinery and equipment	$ 92,675.83	
Less Allowance for depreciation	19,948.83	72,727.00
Motor trucks	$ 7,620.00	
Less Allowance for depreciation	2,955.00	4,665.00
Salesroom furniture	$ 2,529.81	
Less Allowance for depreciation	878.70	1,651.11
General office furniture	$ 1,845.62	
Less Allowance for depreciation	580.74	1,264.88
Total property, plant, and equipment		183,893.74
		$337,712.49

Liabilities and Capital

CURRENT LIABILITIES:

Notes payable	$ 5,000.00	
Accounts payable	16,841.20	
Accrued expenses	3,986.94	
Total current liabilities		$ 25,828.14

LONG-TERM DEBT:

Mortgage payable		15,000.00
CHARLES WATSON, CAPITAL		296,884.35
		$337,712.49

23. Cost Accounting

LET US NOW consider the significance of the item *cost of goods manufactured*. With respect to the illustrative case of Charles Watson in Chapter 22, of what significance is it to the management that the cost of goods manufactured during 1956 is $334,954.97?

The total cost of the goods manufactured during a year is of value only in the computation of the cost of the goods sold, as on page 159, and thus the gross profit on sales, as on page 158. By itself, the total cost of the goods manufactured is too complex a figure and is obtained too late (after a year's operations have been completed) to be useful for managerial purposes.

UNIT COSTS

The cost of the goods manufactured is of great value in the management of a manufacturing business when analyzed into *unit costs* of production. For example, take the case of a certain bakery in which the cost of production of 1,000,000 loaves of bread during 1956 is $437,985.26. Then, dividing $437,985.26 by 1,000,000, the cost of production of each loaf of bread, or unit cost of production, is approximately $.0438. Such a unit cost is useful in comparing production results from period to period. If the cost of production for 1955 was $.0396, the indicated rise in cost would have to be given consideration by the management with a view to either attempting to reduce costs or to increase selling prices, or both. Thus unit costs aid management in exercising control over production and in planning selling prices.

But the unit cost of production as computed above is not satisfactory. In this computation there is the assumption that the prices of materials, of direct labor, and of the various types of manufacturing expenses were uniform during the year, a condition that usually does not exist. If, instead of making one computation for the entire year, it were possible to make separate computations by months it would most likely be found that the unit cost was different for each month. For example, it might be found that the unit cost for January was $.0372, for July $.0413, and for December $.0442. Such more frequent cost infor-

161

mation would enable the management to exercise constant control over cost of production.

PRODUCT COSTS

Further, the foregoing discussion has assumed that the bakery produces only one product: uniform loaves of bread. But this is not to be expected. It is more likely that there would be at least three kinds of bread: white, rye, and whole wheat, each of which would have a different cost of production. Also, the bakery might produce the loaves in different sizes. And in addition it might produce rolls, cakes, and other products. The management would, therefore, require cost information regarding each product.

DEPARTMENTAL COSTS

Still more information, however, is needed. Let us assume that the bakery is divided into three departments: Mixing, Baking, and Wrapping. Management desires to know the cost of production in each department, both in total and by units, and classified into the elements of material, labor, and manufacturing overhead. By the use of these data it is possible to study variations of cost in all phases of production as a basis for managerial decisions.

COST ACCOUNTING

Since management requires information regarding cost of production not only more frequently than once a year, but also analyzed into material, labor, and overhead costs, by products and units of product, and also by departments, the total cost of the goods manufactured during a year as obtained by general accounting procedure is not useful for managerial purposes. Therefore, in order to provide management with the information required by it, certain accounting procedures have been developed. These are known as *cost accounting*.

It may be said that the starting point of cost accounting procedures is that the three inventory accounts—Materials, Work in Process, and Finished Goods—are used as control accounts. These accounts control subsidiary ledgers or records which constitute perpetual inventories of materials, work in process, and finished goods.

MATERIALS LEDGER

In the materials or stores ledger there is an account with each kind of material carried in the storeroom. Whenever material is received the account with that particular kind of material is debited and when material is issued, that is, placed in process, the appropriate account is credited. So that at any time when all receipts and issues of materials

162

have been recorded, the materials ledger provides a record of the materials in the storeroom.

When the finished product emerges from the manufacturing processes it is placed in the stockroom. At this time a record of the finished goods is made in the finished goods or stock ledger by a debit to the account with the type of goods manufactured and when goods are sold the appropriate account is credited. Accordingly, the finished goods ledger is a perpetual record of the goods in stock ready for sale.

FINISHED
GOODS
LEDGER

The work in process ledger is more complicated than either the materials or finished goods ledger for this ledger acts as a record of the accumulated costs of the materials, labor, and indirect expenses that constitute the cost of production.

WORK IN
PROCESS
LEDGER

It is in the keeping of the record of work in process that important differences in cost accounting methods occur. The methods employed are more or less dependent on the type of business. Two of these methods will now be discussed.

In industries such as clothing, shoes, furniture, and printing, goods are usually manufactured on specific orders. Therefore, the enterprises in these industries use a type of cost accounting that is called *specific order* or *job order* cost accounting.

JOB ORDER
SYSTEM

Under a job order system there is an account or *cost sheet* in the goods in process ledger for each order, or job lot, or batch of product. On this cost sheet there is recorded all the costs of the material, the direct labor, and the estimated indirect manufacturing expenses allocated to that specific order or job. The total is the cost of the job which when divided by the number of units produced gives the unit cost of production.

In industries such as cement, paint, textiles, and chemicals, where there is a continuous mass production of uniform products, a type of cost system is employed known as *process* or *operation* cost accounting.

PROCESS
SYSTEM

Under the process cost accounting method the costs are accumulated in the work in process record by processes or stages in production instead of by jobs. The total of the accumulated costs of the

163

various processes divided by the number of units produced in a period of time such as a month gives the unit cost of production for that period.

GENERAL
LEDGER
ACCOUNTS

It has been shown that in the general accounting type of manufacturing accounting, entries are made in the inventory accounts only once a year to record the final inventories and to close out the initial inventories, just as in a merchandising business. But in the cost accounting type of manufacturing accounting the inventory accounts are used throughout the year to record the flow of costs. At the end of each month a summary of the debit and credit entries in the subsidiary ledgers is posted to the control accounts which, as a result, will record the total of the three inventories given in detail in the subsidiary ledgers.

To illustrate, suppose that the records of a manufacturing enterprise for a certain month show:

Initial inventories	
Materials	$47,295
Work in process	6,421
Finished goods	63,960
Materials	
Purchases	16,389
Placed in process	24,307
Direct labor	13,500
Manufacturing expenses	
Incurred	5,480
Applied to production	4,250
Deferred	1,230
Cost of goods finished	41,625
Goods sold (cost)	57,392
Final inventories	
Materials	39,377
Work in process	6,853
Finished goods	48,193

The flow of costs through the general ledger accounts of this business is illustrated in the diagram on page 165.

ROLE OF
COST
ACCOUNTING

From the foregoing it is seen that cost accounting is an analytical supplement to general accounting, devised for the purpose of obtaining a detailed analysis of certain data shown only in total in the general accounting records.

164

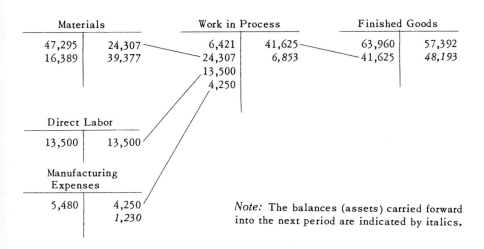

Materials	
47,295	24,307
16,389	39,377

Work in Process	
6,421	41,625
24,307	6,853
13,500	
4,250	

Finished Goods	
63,960	57,392
41,625	48,193

Direct Labor	
13,500	13,500

Manufacturing Expenses	
5,480	4,250
	1,230

Note: The balances (assets) carried forward into the next period are indicated by italics.

The principles of cost accounting are applicable not only to *production costs* but also to *distribution costs,* that is, the costs involved in selling the products produced. Analyses are made with respect to the different classes of sales and also with respect to the sales functions, such as solicitation, advertising, warehousing, and delivery. Information regarding the cost of the various phases of the sales effort is just as important to management as that of the cost of production.

V.

UNDERSTANDING THE ACCOUNTING DATA

24. The Stuff the Accounting Data Are Made Of

THE WORD *theory* is used in various ways. A theory may be an explanation of phenomena, as, for example, Lavoisier's theory of combustion and Adam Smith's theory of moral sentiments. It may be a hypothesis to be used as a basis of thought in seeking an explanation. Also, it may be used in the sense of the principles of a given body of knowledge. Accounting is not a phenomenon to be explained; nor does one need a hypothesis for the purpose of explaining it. When the word *theory* is used in connection with accounting it refers to the principles on which the art is based.

ACCOUNTING THEORY

In order to differentiate briefly between art and science, it may be said that a science is an exact and systematic body of knowledge of a certain subject, whereas an art is the skillful and systematic arrangement of means for the attainment of some end. Science is concerned with knowledge, art with doing.

ACCOUNTING AN ART

Art divides itself into the aesthetic or fine arts and the industrial or mechanical arts. The mechanical arts are governed by more or less exact rules, whereas the aesthetic arts, although using rules, tend to transcend all rule.

Accounting is an art of the mechanical type. Its end is the gathering of data concerning a business enterprise. Because the technique of the art of accounting is exact, as, for example, the matter of balancing of debits and credits, it is often mistaken for a science.

In order to appreciate the nature of accounting and its results, it is imperative to understand the principles on which it operates. These consist of: (1) an axiom, (2) conventions, and (3) postulates.

The principles of accounting start with the axiom that the total of the assets is equal to the total of the equities or interests in the assets, that is, the liabilities and the capital. To state it in simple language: the total of the wealth in a business is equal to what was put into it by the two possible sources, owners and creditors. This self-evident truth is accepted as soon as it is stated and requires no elab-

THE AXIOM

169

oration. It is the keystone on which rests the most fundamental technique of accounting, the system of debit and credit.

CONVENTIONS   Having based the technique of their art on an axiom, the accountants proceed to employ a series of conventional rules to facilitate the application of the technique. In the case of debit and credit there is a conventional system by which, for example, an asset account is debited when that asset increases. The system could easily be changed by reversing the debits and credits and thus crediting an asset account when the asset increases.

Another example of an accounting convention is afforded by the amortization of fixed asset costs (depreciation). The ideal procedure would consist of assigning to the revenue of each accounting period the exact portion of the cost that had been dissipated during the period. Since, however, it is not possible to calculate such cost exactly, the conventional procedure in use has been adopted to facilitate the accounting processes.

The pricing of inventories presents an additional example of conventional procedure. Among the accepted rules one finds that of pricing the inventory on the basis of cost or market, whichever is lower. This convention is not entirely logical since the loss taken in case of a market decline may never be realized, and, on the other hand, a gain ignored may be realized. In spite of its apparent lack of logic, it has been accepted because of its conservatism.

Since the accounting processes consist of conventional procedures, accounting is in sharp contrast with a science such as physics in which the rules or laws consist of generalizations of the behavior of natural phenomena. The physicists cannot change the law of gravity but the accountants can readily change the rules of depreciation and inventory pricing.

In some respects the *modus operandi* of accounting is akin to that of the drama. Upon buying a theater ticket you make an agreement with the management to observe the conventions of the drama. And when, for example, on the stage the action takes place in a room that has only three walls instead of four and the persons in that room have the strange habit of talking toward the side of the room minus a wall, you do not demand a refund of the admission charge because the scene is not true to life. You naturally observe the conventions of the drama. Shakespeare pleads for the observance of these conventions in his prologue to *Henry V* when he says:

170

... But pardon, gentles all,
The flat unraised spirit that hath dar'd
On this unworthy scaffold to bring forth
So great an object: can this cockpit hold
The vasty fields of France? or may we cram
Within this wooden O the very casques
That did affright the air of Agincourt?
O, pardon! since a crooked figure may
Attest in little place a million;
And let us, ciphers to this great accompt,
On your imaginary forces work.

In similar manner it is necessary to understand and observe the conventions of accounting when using the accounting data.

POSTULATES

The conventional procedures are implemented by the use of various postulates or assumptions. One of these is the "going concern" postulate, according to which it is assumed that the enterprise for which the accounting is performed will remain in business. If the enterprise were planning to liquidate, the conventional record would no longer be valid. In such case, for example, the assets would have to be stated on the cash realizable basis.

Then there is the postulate to the effect that the purchasing power or "value" of money is constant. Accounting does not differentiate among the dollars of various years having different purchasing power. As far as accounting is concerned, a dollar is a dollar, no matter whether the transaction it measures took place in 1929, 1931, 1939, 1945, or 1956. This is, of course, an assumption that is contrary to fact. Because of important price changes in recent years, this assumption has been the subject of considerable criticism.

JUDGMENT

The two elementary illustrations given above—that of the depreciation of fixed assets and that of the pricing of inventories—serve to show that accounting operates on the basis of conventional rules, many of which are dictated by expediency. To this should be added the fact that in order to apply the conventional rules it is necessary for the accountant to exercise judgment.

With respect to depreciation the accountant must not only select the proper rate to be used but also the method by which it is to be applied. He might use what is called the *straight-line* method by which each year's depreciation is based on the original cost. This is by far

171

the most common method. But he might compute the depreciation on the original cost less the accumulated depreciation to date, or book value. Also, with such an asset as machinery he might compute the depreciation on the basis of the number of hours the machine was used during the period or the volume of goods it had turned out.

Then, with respect to inventories, in applying the *cost or market, whichever is lower* rule, the accountant might proceed on the assumption that the cost prices of the first goods placed in stock were assigned first, or he might assume that the last prices were assigned first. The selection of the method from among the alternatives depends on the judgment of the accountant in each particular case.

THEORY
VERSUS
PRINCIPLES

Since accounting is a matter of doing, its theory consists largely of generalizations of how accountants do their work. It is, therefore, preferable to refer to these generalizations as principles rather than theory in order to avoid the connotations that the word *theory* conveys of hypotheses or explanations of phenomena—matters that are foreign to accounting.

For convenience, in academic circles the discussion of principles is sometimes referred to as *theory* and the working of problems as *laboratory*.

CONCLUSION

Accounting is thus an art based on an axiom and operated on a series of conventions and postulates that are applied by the use of judgment. This judgment, however, is not arbitrary but is an informed one that has a background of experience of the accounting profession.

It is, accordingly, important to recognize that as a result of the procedures used in the compilation of the accounting data they are not simply facts but a combination of facts, conventions, postulates, and judgments. The judgments affect them materially.

172

25. Costs and Expenses

ACCOUNTING IS largely a matter of accounting for costs. Business costs may be divided into three categories: (1) the cost of the fixed assets, (2) the cost of the goods or materials purchased for resale, or manufacture and sale, and (3) the cost of the selling, general, and administrative activities.

Business costs are incurred for the purpose of earning income. Accordingly, in the course of time the costs are assigned to income; that is, they are deducted from the income they were instrumental in earning. This process has in recent times been described as *matching costs with revenue*.

Costs that have been assigned as deductions from income (revenue) are classified as *expenses*. Those costs that have not been assigned to income are classified as *assets*. That is, the costs of goods or services that have been incurred and used up, or have *expired,* are expenses, and *unexpired* costs are assets. Thus assets, with the exception of cash and claims to cash such as receivables and securities, are unexpired costs.

The assigning of costs as deductions from income is the central problem of accounting. It is particularly in this phase of the accountant's work, which is done in the process of adjusting and closing the books, that use is made of the conventions and postulates of the art and of professional judgment.

It has been demonstrated in the preceding chapters how the fixed asset costs are deducted from income by conventional depreciation methods. The depreciation expense, as found in the income statement, is the expired portion of the cost; the net asset amount, as shown in the balance sheet, is the unexpired portion of the cost.

The expired portion of the cost of the goods or materials purchased for resale, or manufacture and sale, is found in the income statement as cost of goods sold. The unexpired portion is the inventory as stated in the balance sheet.

In similar manner, the expired portion of the selling, general, and administrative costs is listed as expense in the income statement.

173

The unexpired portion is shown among the assets as prepaid expenses or deferred charges.

NATURE OF THE NET INCOME FIGURE

Since in performing the process of matching the costs with the income to which they are applicable the accountant makes use of conventional procedures, implemented by assumptions or postulates, and applied by the use of judgment, the figure designated in the income statement as *net income for the period* is not an absolute measure of the net income but rather the opinion of the accountant who did the job. Within reasonable limits, if another accountant had performed the work, the net income figure might be a different one. In this respect, the accountant's opinion is comparable with opinions in other professions, such as a physician's diagnosis and a judge's decision.

It should, however, be pointed out that since all costs must eventually be accounted for, none are lost in the process of allocation to income. The differences in opinion affect only the amounts to be assigned to specific periods on the accrual basis of accounting. Any costs not allocated to a period will be allocated to future periods and, *vice versa,* costs allocated to a period under review will not be allocated to future periods.

NATURE OF ASSET FIGURES

It follows from the foregoing that the stated dollar amounts of most of the assets, being the deferred or unexpired costs of the assets, have no relation to the value of these assets in the business world. The market value of assets is a matter with which the accountant as such is not concerned. His job is that of the apportionment of the asset costs to income. However, the businessman is often interested in knowing the market value of his assets. To obtain such information he should consult another kind of professional man known as an appraiser.

VALUE

What is *value?* Most persons who have not had the matter brought to their attention assume that everything has an absolute money value and that if you go to the appropriate source you can determine such value. This, of course, is not so.

Value may be defined as the money amount assigned to a particular object for a particular purpose and this value will change as the purpose of the valuation changes. Take, for example, a building. It has a market value in the real estate market; it has a replacement value (the cost of constructing a building just like it); an assessed value for tax

174

purposes; if owned by a public utility it might be assigned a value in connection with rate-making, and, finally, it would have an accounting or book value. All of these values would probably be different. There is no such thing as a "real," intrinsic, or absolute value. This shows why the accountants have need of a conventional rule to carry on their work; also that in order to understand a balance sheet it is essential to be familiar with the conventions of accounting.

Economists hold that one of the things the businessman should do is to compute the interest on the sum invested or about to be invested in a business at the rate that could be earned by an investment in "safe" securities. They explain that when such a calculation is made in advance of investment in a business it is for the purpose of comparing this interest with the estimate of what the business will yield in order to determine whether it would be preferable to make an investment in "safe" securities or in the business. Economists also hold that in the case of a business already in operation the owner should calculate the "safe" interest on his capital and consider it one of the costs of doing business since he has sacrificed this sum by not having made the investment in the "safe" securities.

ECONOMIC COSTS AND ACCOUNTING COSTS

Accountants, however, hold that the calculation of interest on capital is not acceptable because accounting records only what has actually occurred or is expected to occur. Since no money was received or will be received in such a form that it may be regarded in the nature of interest on capital such interest should not be given consideration.

In similar manner when a business is in the form of an individual proprietorship or partnership and the owner or partner spends time working in the business, economists hold that he should make a reasonable deduction from the income of the business for the salary that he would have earned if employed elsewhere and that he has sacrificed by spending his time in the business. Accounting, however, does not permit such a deduction from income since it recognizes no subdivision of the income into categories of interest on capital, salary, and pure profit.

But the fact remains that the prudent businessman does need to take interest on capital and remuneration for his labor into consideration in order to plan his economic behavior: whether to continue the operation of his business or to invest his money in other channels and to seek employment elsewhere. It is logically sound as a matter of business reasoning although not satisfactory for accounting purposes.

175

There is no actual conflict between the teachings of economics and accounting. Each discipline treats the various matters in which there appears to be a conflict with a different purpose in mind: the economists to explain economic behavior, the accountants to expound the rules of accounting with respect to the determination of the net income of a business. The economist is concerned essentially with the point of view of the administration of a business enterprise and so makes estimates of what is likely to occur; the accountant, on the other hand, records only what has actually occurred or is expected to occur. Lack of an appreciation of the difference in purpose has led to confusion.

26. Accounting and the Price Level

WE HAVE SEEN that among the postulates of accounting there is the tacit assumption, contrary to fact, that the value each dollar recorded in the books had at the time the transaction it measured took place was exactly the same as that of all the other dollars in the accounting record. This assumption is maintained throughout the entire process of the mechanics of accounting from the original entries for transactions to the final statements. It has been found necessary to adopt this postulate in order to facilitate the accounting processes. Unless the businessman is aware of this assumption, he may arrive at fallacious conclusions when he compares the financial statements prepared for him by his accountant from year to year. THE MONEY POSTULATE

To illustrate, let it be assumed that the sales of a certain business for three years are stated in its income statements as follows:

> First year..............................$16,575
> Second year........................... 17,350
> Third year............................. 18,653

If during these years the price level had risen, it is most likely that at least part of the increase in the sales figure is the effect of the rise in prices, or, in other words, the decline in the value, or purchasing power, of the dollar. It would be possible to get a better interpretation of the status of the business if the distortion of the results of operations caused by the change in the price level could be removed.

In 1936, Henry W. Sweeney published his pioneering work, *Stabilized Accounting,* in which he outlined a technique for the conversion of the dollar amounts in financial statements into dollars of equal purchasing power. There was no great interest in the book at the time because no considerable change was taking place in the price level. However, since World War II the problem has come to the fore because of the sharp rise in the price level; and some accountants believe that it would be well if the financial statements in traditional form might be supplemented by statements in which the data are converted into uniform purchasing-power units, so that, the disturbing factor of ADJUSTMENT FOR PRICE LEVEL CHANGES change in the unit of measurement having been eliminated, management might be able to see more clearly certain facts in the statements that are now obscured.

Applying the index-number technique to the hypothetical case above, let it be assumed that the average of the price level during the second and third years was 110 per cent and 125 per cent, respectively, of that of the first year. The price index for the three years, taking the first year as the base, then is:

First year 100%
Second year............................. 110
Third year................................. 125

The sales for the second and third years may be converted to the price level of the first year and the figures for the three years thus placed on a comparable basis by dividing the sales of the second and third years by the indexes of the price level in those years. The results are:

First year $16,575
Second year 15,773
Third year............................ 14,922

The application of index numbers to the accounting figures shows that the sales volume of the business, measured in terms of the dollars of the first year, did not increase, but declined.

In similar manner other items of the financial statements may be adjusted.

PROBLEM OF A SUITABLE INDEX

At first blush the matter of adjustment of the accounting figures appears quite simple: all you need to do is to apply the index number. But what index number? Shall it be a *general index* of prices or a *specific index* that measures prices in the industry in which the enterprise under consideration is engaged?

It is not to be expected that any one index number of general prices would be suitable in all cases, for it is known that price level changes do not affect all industries in a uniform manner; there are what the economist calls "leads" and "lags." This would indicate the need for specific indexes, at least for such industries as do not follow the general pattern of prices. It will also be necessary to examine whether all branches of what might be called an "industry" are similarly affected by the movement of prices.

Then, too, there is the question whether the same index is suit-

178

able for adjustment of all items in the statements. It often happens that changes in production costs and in selling, general, and administrative costs are quite different from those in selling prices. There is also the problem of the changes in the prices of construction of facilities and acquisition of equipment.

Although it would be desirable to have available statements converted into units of equal purchasing power, their preparation will not be feasible until acceptable index numbers have been developed. There can be no doubt that the task of developing such index numbers is a formidable one. In fact, little progress has been made in this direction by research workers engaged in attempts to produce index numbers.

The price level problem is not new to management. No alert business executive ever accepted the accounting results without what he calls a "grain of salt" in which he includes mental adjustments for the fluctuations in the purchasing power of money. This, in fact, has been the common practice from time immemorial. The suggestion of an index number technique is an attempt to make the adjustments more precise by the use of ingenious statistical devices. These, however, may possibly produce results farther away from reality than the crude mental adjustments of a keen business executive.

PRACTICAL TREATMENT OF THE PROBLEM

Unfortunately, as a matter of practical application, no matter how good an index might be invented its value to management will be doubtful because of the delay in obtaining the index numbers and applying them to the conventional data. Management needs information as soon as possible,—in fact, even before the conventional statements can be prepared. It would, therefore, seem that at best any figures adjusted for price level changes will not be available until after they can be of use for managerial purposes.

179

27. Current Problems in Income Measurement

THE RISE IN the price level since World War II has caused confusion in the interpretation of the results of accounting as shown in financial statements, particularly the income statement. This has brought forth various suggestions in favor of departures from traditional procedure for determining income, some of which have been adopted whereas others have not.

STATEMENT OF
THE PROBLEM

The crux of the matter is found in the question: Since the revenue is measured in current dollars, why not measure the deductions from revenue in terms of the same dollars?

Some of the deductions from revenue are measured in current dollars as, for example, most of the selling, general, and administrative expenses, with the possible exception of items deferred from previous periods which usually are negligible. However, two of the deductions from revenue that are important and that in a period of changing prices are usually not measured in current dollars are the cost of the goods sold and the depreciation of the fixed assets.

COST OF GOODS
SOLD

In a period of rising prices the cost of the goods sold may not be measured in current dollars because the goods may have been purchased at various prices, most of them lower than the current ones. And if in taking goods out of stock their costs are recorded beginning with the prices of those put in first, known as the "first-in, first-out" (FIFO) method, the stated cost of goods sold will be on a basis lower than the current price level.

To bring the cost of goods sold up to the current level many accountants have adopted the "last-in, first-out" (LIFO) method whereby prices are assigned as cost of goods sold beginning with the price paid for the last goods placed in stock. The effect of this procedure is to reflect the latest prices in the cost of goods sold.

It does not follow under the LIFO method that the last goods placed in stock are taken out first. The advocates of this method explain that it does not matter which of any identifiable goods are taken

180

out first since in the accounting they are not interested in the flow of goods but in the *flow of costs*. Thus an item placed in the storeroom first may be taken out first but the issue may be priced at the latest cost figure. The LIFO method has gained wide adoption because it has been accepted by the Treasury Department for income tax purposes.

The traditional method of basing the depreciation charge on the cost of the fixed assets does not reflect the current price level but the price levels at which the fixed assets were purchased; and these may be very different from the current ones. The proponents of stating the deduction from revenue for depreciation in current dollars suggest that it be computed on current replacement prices. This, however, presents difficulties. **DEPRECIATION**

Depreciation accounting is the process of assigning to revenue costs that have been recorded in the books. So the question asked by the conservative accountants is: "How may we assign to revenue costs which do not exist in the books? We cannot assign more dollars than were recorded." The advocates of the "depreciation on replacement price" method have suggested various schemes for treating the problem, one of which is that the fixed assets be reappraised periodically with a credit to a Capital Adjustment account—a sort of quasi-reorganization. This presents the time-honored question of the feasibility of making periodic reappraisals: the cost involved, and the fact that the reappraisal will reflect merely the opinion of one appraiser which may differ considerably from another's.

Then there arises the question of what is to become of the credit balance in this Capital Adjustment account. One answer is that if the period of rising prices should be followed by one of falling prices the process would be reversed, the assets being written down with a debit to the Capital Adjustment account, resulting in the reduction of the depreciation charge to the then current price level.

Although the LIFO device for bringing the cost of goods sold in line with current prices has received recognition as acceptable procedure by the accounting profession, encouraged by the attitude of the Treasury Department, no scheme for stating depreciation in current dollars has been generally accepted. The solution of the cost of goods sold problem is much simpler than that of depreciation because it involves merely the order in which recorded costs are to be assigned to revenue. The statement of the depreciation figure in terms of current **PRESENT STATUS OF THE PROBLEM**

181

dollars in a period of rising prices requires the addition of dollar amounts to the fixed asset records in a manner that has until now been considered unacceptable.

The problem of the purchasing power of money is economic and one which the economists themselves have not succeeded in solving. However, it continues to be given careful consideration by the accounting profession.

THE REALISM OF ACCOUNTING

It was pointed out in Chapter 25 that accounting gives recognition only to what has actually occurred in a business enterprise. The consideration of what would be the status of various phases of the activity of a business if the management had followed a policy other than that which was followed is foreign to accounting. It is, however, relevant in the matter of managerial decisions where the weighing of alternatives of behavior takes place. Thus, for example, the consideration by an individual whether to invest in "safe" bonds or in a business enterprise is an important matter to him; but there is no place in accounting for the weighing of such alternatives. Accounting is concerned only with what actually was done. This adherence to recognition of only what has actually occurred is a postulate of accounting that may be called the "actuality" or "realism" postulate.

In some cases the current prices have moved to a higher level than those of any of the prices actually paid. It has been suggested that in such cases the replacement cost or "next-in-first-out" (NIFO) basis be used. This, however, violates the actuality postulate since no goods were purchased at the prices assigned and so is not acceptable to the accountant.

It would appear that the computation of depreciation on replacement cost is unacceptable for the same reason. The dollars of actual cost are a reality to the accountant; the dollars of replacement cost are not real from his point of view, since no assets were purchased at the replacement prices.

The accounting profession would apparently be willing to consider the adjustment of the actual cost figures if it could be shown that such adjustment produces valid results. This, however, has not yet been demonstrated. On the other hand, there are economists who believe that the realism of the accountants is a mistaken one, for it has not succeeded in giving adequate effect to price level changes.

VI.

MATTERS PECULIAR TO THE FORMS OF OWNERSHIP ORGANIZATION

28. Partnerships: Formation

IT HAS ALREADY been stated that a business in the partnership form is owned by more than one person, usually a small number. It should be added that the object of the association of the partners is for profit. Although no governmental sanction is required in order to organize a partnership, local laws may require the registration of the partnership.

Since there is no difference in the matter of accounting for the income, expenses, assets, or liabilities of an individual proprietorship, partnership, or corporation, the problem of accounting for the partnership is one of accounting for its capital.

The partnership is a contractual relationship; therefore, the law of contracts applies. The contract may be either oral or written but it is advisable to have a written agreement in order to avoid disputes. When a written agreement is drawn up it is known as the *articles of copartnership.*

It is important that the partnership agreement cover all points concerning which misunderstandings might arise. Among those of a general nature are: the name of the firm, the nature of the business, the place of business, when the partnership agreement shall go into effect, and the method of settling disputes. Those stipulations that affect the accounting and that are of particular interest in the present discussion are:

The capital contribution of each partner.
The withdrawal of funds by the partners.
The division of the profits and losses.
The conditions under which the partnership may be dissolved.

Broadly speaking, the admission of a new partner or the withdrawal of a partner dissolves the partnership and a new partnership must be formed to carry on the business.

185

LEGAL RELA-
TIONSHIPS

Agency. A partner is the agent of the other partners. When he acts for the firm, within the scope of the normal activities of the business, his acts are binding upon all the other partners. Thus the law of agency enters into all partnership relations.

Unlimited liability. Each partner is individually liable for all the debts of the partnership to the full extent of his private fortune, except for such property as is exempted by the bankruptcy laws. However, a partner who has paid the claims of creditors in excess of his share may recover from the other partners.

A partner's liability may be limited to the capital he has contributed to the partnership. Such a partner is called a *limited partner*. Partnerships with limited partners are permitted under the laws of certain states. The statutes usually require, however, a certain number of general partners who have unlimited liability, ordinarily two. A limited partner may take no active part in the management of the business and it must be publicly known that he is a limited partner.

RECORDING THE
CAPITAL CON-
TRIBUTION

The capital contribution of a partner is recorded in the same manner as is the capital of an individual proprietorship. In this respect the only distinction is that in an individual proprietorship there is only one Capital account whereas in a partnership there are more than one. Naturally, there is a Drawing account to record the withdrawals of each partner.

If at the inception of a partnership there is merely an investment of cash by the partners the opening or *pro forma* entry is simple. For example:

Cash	10,000.00	
A. L. Cooper, Capital		10,000.00
To record the investment of A. L. Cooper.		

Cash	5,000.00	
M. S. Goodwin, Capital		5,000.00
To record the investment of M. S. Goodwin.		

But when the investment consists of several assets and perhaps some liabilities, as in the case of the merger of two enterprises, the entry is more elaborate:

Cash	2,500.00	
Accounts receivable	8,000.00	
Furniture and fixtures	1,250.00	
Accounts payable		1,750.00
R. S. Wiley, Capital		10,000.00
To record the investment of R. S. Wiley.		

186

Cash	8,000.00	
Motor truck	2,500.00	
Accounts payable		500.00
T. C. Richards, Capital		10,000.00
To record the investment of T. C. Richards.		

When a partner withdraws funds, as permitted by the partnership agreement, the entry to be made consists of a debit to the partner's Drawing account and a credit to Cash. When a partner takes merchandise from stock his Drawing account is similarly debited, the corresponding credit being to Purchases since the merchandise taken out of stock reduces the amount purchased and available for resale. The merchandise is charged to the partner at cost. **RECORDING WITHDRAWALS**

Sometimes a loan is made by a partner to the partnership. Such loans are credited to a Loan account with the partner. For example, if R. S. Wiley should lend $1,000.00 to the business the entry would be: **LOANS BY PARTNERS**

Cash	1,000.00	
R. S. Wiley, Loan		1,000.00
To record loan by R. S. Wiley.		

In preparing a balance sheet a partner's Loan account may be shown either as a current liability or as an addition to capital, depending on whether or not the loan is to be repaid within the current period.

187

29. Partnerships: Division of Profits

THE BALANCE OF the Profit and Loss account, representing the net income or net loss for the period, is divided in accordance with the partnership agreement. The common method of dividing profits and losses is to divide them equally. In fact, in the absence of any specific agreement regarding the division of profits it is the presumption of the law that they are to be divided equally. But in some cases an equal division of profits would not be equitable: one partner may have made a greater investment, or devotes more time to the business than another. For such reasons an unequal division of the profits may be agreed upon.

Illustrations of five methods of dividing profits will now be given. In these the profits are divided:

Equally.
In the ratio of the capitals at the beginning of the period.
In the average capital ratio.
By allowing salaries to partners and dividing the remainder of the profits equally.
By allowing interest on capitals and dividing the remainder of the profits equally.

In these illustrations it is assumed that all partners have made withdrawals that have been debited to their Drawing accounts. Therefore, each partner's share of the net income is closed into his Drawing account. It should be borne in mind that the balance of the Drawing account, which is the partner's share of the net income less withdrawals, is then closed into his Capital account.

Profits divided equally. A net income of $25,000.00 is to be divided equally between the partners A and B. The entry is:

Profit and loss	25,000.00	
A, Drawing		12,500.00
B, Drawing		12,500.00
To divide net income, ½ to A and ½ to B.		

188

Profits divided in the ratio of capitals at the beginning of the period. A net income of $12,000.00 is to be divided between C and D who at the beginning of the period had capital balances of $60,000.00 and $30,000.00, respectively. The entry is:

Profit and loss	12,000.00	
C, Drawing		8,000.00
D, Drawing		4,000.00
To divide net income, ⅔ to C and ⅓ to D.		

Profits divided in the average capital ratio. A net income of $33,-000.00 is to be divided between E and F.

E's capital on January 1 was $50,000.00. On May 1 he withdrew $10,000.00; and on August 1 he invested $40,000.00.

F's capital on January 1 was $30,000.00. On May 1 he invested $20,000.00; and on August 1 he invested $16,000.00.

The computation of the average investments is made in the following manner:

Average capital of E:

Date	Capital Balance	Months Unchanged	Dollar-Months
Jan. 1	$50,000	4	200,000
May 1	40,000	3	120,000
Aug. 1	80,000	5	400,000
		12	720,000

Average capital, 720,000 ÷ 12 = $60,000.00.

Average capital of F:

Date	Capital Balance	Months Unchanged	Dollar-Months
Jan. 1	$30,000	4	120,000
May 1	50,000	3	150,000
Aug. 1	66,000	5	330,000
		12	600,000

Average capital, 600,000 ÷ 12 = $50,000.00.

The average capital ratio is 6:5, or $\frac{6}{11}$ to $\frac{5}{11}$, which gives $18,-000.00 to E and $15,000.00 to F.

This result may be obtained without computing the average investments by using the ratios of the dollar-months, that is, 720:600, which is the same 6:5 ratio.

The entry for the division of the net income is:

189

```
Profit and loss ................................................................ 33,000.00
    E, Drawing ...........................................................                  18,000.00
    F, Drawing ...........................................................                  15,000.00
    To divide net income, 6/11 to E and 5/11 to F.
```

Profits divided by allowing salaries to partners and dividing the remainder of the profits equally. In order to compensate partners in proportion to ability or time spent in the business, part of the profit may be distributed in the form of a salary. A partner's salary is not an expense of the business, that is, a deduction from income, but is part of the profit-sharing scheme.

The entry for a partner's salary consists of a debit to Profit and Loss and a credit to the partner's Drawing account. The payment to the partner is recorded by a debit to his Drawing account and a credit to Cash.

The salary payments to a partner may be made periodically, say monthly. In such case the debits in his Drawing account for the payments will be offset at the end of the period by the credit representing this portion of his share of the net income.

For example: a net income of $50,000.00 is to be divided between G and H whose profit-sharing agreement provides for annual salaries of $18,000.00 to G and $12,000.00 to H, the remainder of the net income to be divided equally. The entries are:

```
Profit and loss ................................................................ 30,000.00
    G, Drawing ...........................................................                  18,000.00
    H, Drawing ...........................................................                  12,000.00
    To allow salaries for year.

Profit and loss ................................................................ 20,000.00
    G, Drawing ...........................................................                  10,000.00
    H, Drawing ...........................................................                  10,000.00
    To divide remainder of net income equally.
```

Profits divided by allowing interest on capitals and dividing the remainder of the profits equally. When there is considerable difference in the amounts of the capitals of the partners it is often agreed to allow interest on the capitals in order to compensate the partners in proportion to their investment. The remainder of the net income may then be divided equally.

As in the case of salaries of partners, interest on capital is not an expense of the business but part of the profit-sharing scheme.

For example: a net income of $10,000.00 is to be divided between I and J whose capitals are $80,000.00 and $20,000.00, respectively, and who have agreed to allow interest at the rate of 6 per cent per annum on capitals and to divide the remainder of the net income equally. The entries are:

Profit and loss 6,000.00		
I, Drawing		4,800.00
J, Drawing		1,200.00
To allow interest on capitals.		
Profit and loss 4,000.00		
I, Drawing		2,000.00
J, Drawing		2,000.00
To divide remainder of net income equally.		

The interest on loans by partners to the partnership should not be confused with interest on capitals. The interest on loans, in contrast with interest on capitals, is an expense of the business and should be debited to Interest Expense in the same manner as interest paid to outsiders. **INTEREST ON PARTNERS' LOANS**

Whether or not interest is to be allowed on partners' loans is a matter subject to agreement. In the absence of an agreement to the contrary it is presumed that interest will be allowed at the legal rate.

191

30. Partnerships: Admission and Retirement of Partners

THERE ARE TWO ways in which a prospective partner may acquire an interest, or equity, in a partnership: (1) he may *purchase an interest* from one or more of the existing partners; or (2) he may *make an investment* of money or property.

PURCHASING AN
INTEREST

If a partner is admitted by purchasing an interest there will be no increase in the partnership's assets. The payment for the acquisition of the interest is made to one or more of the existing partners personally. And the accounting record of the transaction will consist of a transfer of capital by a debit to one or more of the existing Capital accounts and a credit to a new Capital account for the incoming partner.

For example, if partners K and L have capitals of $4,000.00 and $8,000.00, respectively, and M purchases the interest of K, the entry is:

```
K, Capital............................................................... 4,000.00
    M, Capital ......................................................          4,000.00
    To record sale of K's interest to M.
```

The payment for the purchase is a private matter between K and M. M might pay $4,000.00 for the interest or he might pay some other sum.

If M should purchase one quarter of the interest of each K and L the entry would be:

```
K, Capital............................................................... 1,000.00
L, Capital............................................................... 2,000.00
    M, Capital ......................................................          3,000.00
    To record sale of a quarter interest to M.
```

The capitals are now: K, $3,000.00; L, $6,000.00; and M, $3,000.00.

MAKING AN
INVESTMENT

If a partner is admitted by making an investment the assets of the partnership will be increased by the amount of such investment. The accounting record of the transaction will, therefore, consist of a debit to Cash or other asset account and a credit to a Capital account for the new partner.

192

At the time of admission of a new partner it will have to be decided: (1) what shall be the total of the new capital, and (2) what shall be the new partner's share in that capital (usually expressed in the form of a fraction).

Before deciding upon the amount of the new capital it may be desired to include among the assets of the partnership one known as *goodwill*. If a business has earnings greater than what are considered average earnings, it is said to possess goodwill or excess earning power. Excess earning power is obviously a good and valuable thing for a business to possess and should be taken into consideration when it is being determined what a prospective partner shall invest in order to proportion or match his investment with those of the existing partners.

Just how the goodwill shall be measured in terms of money usually reduces itself to a matter of bargaining. But having been agreed upon, the goodwill may be recorded as an asset.

Since goodwill is something that has been acquired through the operation of the business it is regarded in the nature of a form of profit. Therefore, when the account Goodwill is debited in order to record this asset the corresponding credit is to the Capital accounts of the existing partners, divided in the profit-and-loss-sharing ratio, unless some other division is agreed upon.

Goodwill is one of the assets known as *intangible assets*. In a balance sheet these assets are placed in a section the position of which follows that of the fixed assets. Other intangible assets that may appear in a balance sheet are patents, copyrights, trade-marks, and franchises.

A series of cases will now be discussed in order to illustrate, under various circumstances, the accounting for the admission of a new partner making an investment to obtain an interest.

Case 1. No goodwill recognized. The partners N and O have capitals of $20,000.00 and $10,000.00, respectively. They agree to admit P, upon the payment of $10,000.00, to a one-fourth interest in a total capital of $40,000.00.

The entry for the admission of P is:

```
Cash ...................................................................... 10,000.00
    P, Capital ........................................................            10,000.00
        To admit P to a one-fourth interest.
```

The capitals are now: N, $20,000.00; O, $10,000.00; and P, $10.-000.00; or a total of $40,000.00, of which P's $10,000.00 is one fourth.

193

Case 2. Goodwill of old firm recognized and recorded. The partners Q and R have capitals of $30,000.00 and $20,000.00, respectively. They agree to admit S, upon the payment of $20,000.00, to a one-fifth interest in a total capital of $100,000.00.

Since $20,000.00 is one fifth of the proposed capital, the investment by S will give him the agreed share in the capital. But after S makes his investment the total capital will be only $70,000.00. It is short of the agreed total by $30,000.00, which must be the amount of the goodwill it is intended to record.

The entries for the admission of S are:

Goodwill...	30,000.00	
Q, Capital...		15,000.00
R, Capital...		15,000.00
To record goodwill of Q and R.		
Cash	20,000.00	
S, Capital...		20,000.00
To admit S to a one-fifth interest.		

The capitals are now: Q, $45,000.00; R, $35,000.00; and S, $20,-000.00; or a total of $100,000.00, of which S's $20,000.00 is one fifth.

Because the profit-sharing ratio is not stated, an equal division of the goodwill is assumed. If, however, the profits were shared in the capital ratio of three fifths and two fifths, the goodwill would be divided $18,000.00 to Q, and $12,000.00 to R.

Sometimes in a case as this the amount of the goodwill is stated and not the sum to be paid by the incoming partner. The payment is computed in the following manner:

Original capital..	$50,000.00
Goodwill to be added	30,000.00
$4/5$ of new capital....................................	$80,000.00
$1/5$ of new capital....................................	$20,000.00

Case 3. Goodwill of old firm recognized but not recorded. Although the goodwill or earning power of a business may be reasonably measured by the sum recorded at the time a partner is admitted, it cannot be expected that the earning power will remain constant. Therefore, since the amount of goodwill recorded has no definite significance subsequent to the partner's admission, it is often preferred not to record the goodwill although it is taken into consideration in computing the payment to be made by the incoming partner.

If the partners Q and R mentioned in case 2 should desire not to record the goodwill the total capital of the new partnership would be $30,000.00 less than the $100,000.00 in that case, or $70,000.00. And a one-fifth interest would be $14,000.00.

The conditions surrounding the admission of S might then be stated in the following manner: S is to be admitted, upon the payment of $20,000.00, to a one-fifth interest in a total capital of $70,000.00. That is, although S pays in $20,000.00 he is to have a capital of only one fifth of $70,000.00, or $14,000.00. This indicates that although no goodwill is to be recorded its existence is recognized and S pays $6,000.00 more than is to be credited in his Capital account because of its existence. The payment of $6,000.00 may be regarded as in the nature of a bonus to Q and R which S is willing to pay in order to obtain an interest in a lucrative business.

As mentioned under case 2, the goodwill might be stated and not the sum to be invested by the incoming partner. His investment would be computed in the same manner as outlined in case 2 since the incoming partner would make the same investment whether or not the goodwill is to be recorded.

The entry for the admission of S under the condition of not recording the goodwill is:

Cash	20,000.00	
S, Capital		14,000.00
Q, Capital		3,000.00
R, Capital		3,000.00
To admit S to a one-fifth interest.		

The capitals are now: Q, $33,000.00; R, $23,000.00; and S, $14,-000.00; or a total of $70,000.00, of which S's $14,000.00 is one fifth.

It might seem that the method of admitting S in case 2 is more favorable to him than that used in case 3 because in case 2 he obtains a larger capital. However, in either case S owns one fifth of the business and it makes no difference whether that interest is stated at $20,000.00 or $14,000.00. The higher figure is caused by the recording of goodwill; but the more conservative practice is not to record it.

Case 4. Goodwill of incoming partner recognized and recorded. It may be regarded in a particular instance that the admission of a certain individual will provide the business with earning power, perhaps because of his professional skill or social connections. Such goodwill should naturally be taken into consideration.

For example, the partners T and U have capitals of $20,000.00

each. They agree to admit W, upon payment of $14,000.00, to a one-third interest in a total capital of $60,000.00.

Since a one-third interest in the new capital is $20,000.00, the old partners have agreed to admit W upon payment of a sum $6,000.00 less than the amount to be credited to his Capital account. This $6,000.00 must be the measure of the goodwill which it is anticipated that W will bring into the enterprise.

The entry for the admission of W is:

Cash	14,000.00	
Goodwill	6,000.00	
W, Capital		20,000.00
To admit W to a one-third interest.		

The capitals are now $20,000.00 each, or a total of $60,000.00 of which W's $20,000.00 is one third.

Case 5. Goodwill of incoming partner recognized but not recorded. If the partners T and U and the incoming partner W mentioned in case 4 should desire not to record the goodwill the total capital of the new partnership would be $6,000.00 less than the $60,000.00 in that case, or $54,000.00. Under these circumstances the matter might be stated thus:

W is to be admitted, upon the payment of $14,000.00, to a one-third interest in a total capital of $54,000.00. That is, although no goodwill is to be recorded its existence is recognized and W is given a capital of $4,000.00 more than he invests. This is effected by a transfer of $4,000.00 from the capital accounts of the old partners; such transfer is in the nature of giving a bonus to W in order to induce him to enter the business.

The entry for the admission of W under these conditions is:

Cash	14,000.00	
T, Capital	2,000.00	
U, Capital	2,000.00	
W, Capital		18,000.00
To admit W to a one-third interest.		

The capitals are now $18,000.00 each, or a total of $54,000.00 of which W's is one third.

RETIREMENT OF A PARTNER

The retirement of a partner may be effected by the sale of his interest to one or more members of the partnership or to one or more outsiders. The sale of a partner's interest to an outsider has already been explained. The sale of a partner's interest to one or more of the existing partners is recorded as a transfer of the retiring partner's capital to one or more of the other partners' Capital accounts.

If a partner withdraws from the firm and is paid for his interest out of the partnership funds, the withdrawal is recorded by a debit to the retiring partner's Capital account and a credit to Cash. However, the matter of goodwill arises in connection with the withdrawal as well as with the admission of a partner since a partner will require to be paid for any excess earning power that he may relinquish.

Case 1. No goodwill recognized. The partners X, Y, and Z have capitals of $3,000.00, $2,000.00, and $1,000.00, respectively, in a total capital of $6,000.00. They share profits and losses equally. Z is to retire and is to be paid for his interest out of the partnership funds. The entry is:

Z, Capital	1,000.00	
Cash		1,000.00
To record the retirement of Z.		

Z might have been paid off with assets other than cash or, as is often the case, he might have been given a promissory note or a series of promissory notes.

The capitals are now: X, $3,000.00; Y, $2,000.00; or a total of $5,000.00.

Case 2. Goodwill recognized and recorded. If in the case of X, Y., and Z it should be agreed that the goodwill of the firm is to be recorded as $3,000.00, the following entries would be made for the withdrawal of Z:

Goodwill	3,000.00	
X, Capital		1,000.00
Y, Capital		1,000.00
Z, Capital		1,000.00
To record goodwill of the firm.		

Z, Capital	2,000.00	
Cash		2,000.00
To record the retirement of Z.		

The capitals would now be: X, $4,000.00; Y, $3,000.00; or a total of $7,000.00.

Case 3. Goodwill recognized but not recorded. If in the case of X, Y, and Z it should be decided not to record the goodwill although it is given recognition, the payment for Z's share of the goodwill would be recorded as a deduction from the capitals of X and Y. The entry for the withdrawal of Z would be:

197

```
Z, Capital.................................................................... 1,000.00
X, Capital....................................................................  500.00
Y, Capital....................................................................  500.00
        Cash .................................................................            2,000.00
    To record the retirement of Z.
```

The capitals would now be: X, $2,500.00; Y, $1,500.00; or a total of $4,000.00.

Case 4. Retiring partner paid less than stated capital. It may be agreed that a retiring partner is to be paid less than the amount of his capital as recorded in his Capital account. In such case the excess of the retiring partner's capital over the sum paid is transferred to the Capital accounts of the remaining partners.

For example, if in the case of X, Y, and Z it should be agreed that Z is to be paid $800.00 for his capital which appears in his Capital account as $1,000.00, the entry would be:

```
Z, Capital.................................................................... 1,000.00
        Cash .................................................................             800.00
        X, Capital..........................................................             100.00
        Y, Capital..........................................................             100.00
    To record the retirement of Z.
```

The capitals would now be: X, $3,100.00; Y, $2,100.00; or a total of $5,200.00.

LIQUIDATION OF A PARTNERSHIP

If the members of a partnership should decide to liquidate or "go out of business" there are two processes necessary: (1) the conversion of the assets into cash, known as *realization,* and (2) the distribution of the cash realized, known as *liquidation.* Although there are two distinct processes that must take place, the entire procedure is commonly referred to as "liquidation."

When the assets of a business are sold it is not probable that the sums realized will be exactly the dollar amounts at which the assets are recorded in the books—which in the case of the fixed assets is the cost less the depreciation allowance. It is most likely that the assets will be sold at figures that are greater or less than the recorded amounts. Therefore, a special account to record profits and losses on realization is usually opened; this is given such a title as Realization Profit and Loss account. The profits are recorded as credits and the losses as debits; and the balance is the profit or loss on realization—a profit if a credit balance and a loss if a debit balance.

198

For example, if furniture and fixtures that cost $2,500.00 and have an accumulated depreciation of $1,500.00 are sold for $800.00, the entry is:

```
Cash .................................................................  800.00
Allowance for depreciation of furniture and fixtures ..  1,500.00
Realization profit and loss............................................  200.00
     Furniture and fixtures ...........................................          2,500.00
   To record the sale of furniture and fixtures.
```

The balance of the Realization Profit and Loss account is distributed to the partners' Capital accounts in the same manner as ordinary profits and losses.

In distributing the cash available for liquidation the sums owed to creditors have priority. The remaining cash is paid to the partners.

At the time of termination of a partnership a partner may have a loan extended to the business or may have a credit balance in his Drawing account. In such case he is entitled to receive payment for these amounts before the liquidation of the capitals. But if there exists any possibility that his Capital account may eventually have a debit balance caused by the losses on realization, the balances of the Drawing and Loan accounts should be transferred to the Capital account. The reason for such procedure is that there exists the legal *right of setoff* according to which a debit balance in a partner's Capital account may be set off against any credit balances in such accounts as his Drawing or Loan accounts, that is, any claim of the partnership against him may be set off against his claims against the partnership.

31. Corporations: Capital

CREATION
OF THE
CORPORATION
CORPORATIONS ARE formed under state statutes (with the exception of certain corporations organized under federal statutes). The persons organizing a corporation, known as the *incorporators,* must make application to the proper officer of the state in which the corporation is to be organized—usually the Secretary of State. Upon completion of the required formalities a *charter* is issued by the state and this evidences the creation of the corporation.

**NATURE OF THE
CORPORATION**
The corporation is an entity created by the state; and since the powers granted to this entity are such as are possessed under the law by human beings, the corporation is regarded as an *artificial person.* This artificial person, however, is separate and distinct from the natural persons who have organized it and any that may later be added to their number.

The partnership offers a sharp contrast to the corporation for the partnership is a group of persons and is not something separate and distinct from the persons who compose it. This is illustrated by the manner in which a corporation and a partnership may act in the courts of law. A corporation, since it is a legal entity, may sue and be sued. However, a partnership, since it is not a legal entity but a group of persons, cannot bring suit or be sued. Any suit of the partnership must be brought by the individuals who compose it and, in like manner, any suit against the partnership must be brought against the individual members of the partnership.

**CHARACTER-
ISTICS OF THE
CORPORATION**
Capital divided into transferable shares. As stated in Chapter 3, the main difference in accounting for the three forms of ownership organization—the individual proprietorship, the partnership, and the corporation—lies in the accounting for the capital. The capital investment in the corporation is divided into shares of capital stock. These are evidenced by *stock certificates* which bear the name of the owner and the number of shares represented by the certificate. These certificates may readily be transferred from one owner to another without

200

disrupting the activities of the enterprise. In contrast to this, as was stated in Chapter 28, the transfer of ownership in a partnership necessitates the formation of a new partnership.

Limited liability of stockholders. In contrast to the unlimited liability of the individual partners for the debts of the partnership, the liability of stockholders of the corporation is limited in most states to payment in full for their shares of the capital stock. That is, when a stockholder has fully paid for his stock he has no further liability to the corporation or to its creditors.

Management. The management of the corporation is vested in the board of directors which is elected by the stockholders. The board usually exercises its powers through officers appointed by it. In a partnership each partner ordinarily has an equal voice in the management.

Distribution of earnings. It has been shown that there is no restriction on the withdrawal of earnings by partners unless special arrangements in this respect have been made. Stockholders of a corporation receive income from the business only when the board of directors has taken formal action to authorize or *declare* a distribution of earnings. Such distribution is called a *dividend*.

CLASSES OF CAPITAL STOCK

The capital stock of a corporation may be divided into various classes, each having certain distinct features. The two main classes are: *common stock* and *preferred stock*. These, however, may have several subdivisions with such titles as *common stock, class A, common stock, class B, first preferred stock, second preferred stock,* and so forth.

PREFERRED STOCK

As the name implies, the preferred stock has certain preferences. The forms of preference most commonly found are preference with respect to dividends and preference with respect to the division of assets in the event of liquidation of the corporation.

When preferred stock has preference with respect to dividends, no dividends may be paid on the common stock unless the dividends are paid on the preferred stock. Preference in liquidation signifies that in liquidation the preferred stockholders would be paid off before the common stockholders.

Preferred stock may be *cumulative* or *noncumulative*. If cumulative, any unpaid dividends, or *dividends in arrears,* accumulate until

201

they are declared and paid, and no dividends may be paid on the common stock until all the accumulated or "passed" dividends on the preferred stock have been paid.

Preferred stock may also be *participating*. That is, it may participate with the common stock in any dividend paid on the common stock above a certain rate. To illustrate, let it be assumed that a certain corporation has issued a 6 per cent preferred stock that participates with the common stock in any dividend paid on the common stock above 8 per cent. Therefore, if at a certain time the dividend paid on the common stock should be one of 10 per cent, there would be paid the regular dividend of 6 per cent on the preferred stock plus an extra participating dividend of 2 per cent.

PAR VALUE
STOCK

Capital stock, both common and preferred, may have a *par value* or may be without par value.

The par value of a share of stock is the amount of the investment, measured in terms of money, that an investor must make in order to become the owner of a share of the stock. The par value is stated both in the corporation's charter and in the stock certificate. The most common par is $100.00.

NO-PAR VALUE
STOCK

There are several types of stock without par value that may be issued under the laws of the various states. The two important types are: (1) stock entirely without monetary designation that may be issued for such investment as may be determined by the board of directors at the time of issue; (2) no-par stock with a *stated value* which sets a minimum investment to be received by the corporation upon issuance.

The first type may be regarded as a "pure" no-par stock while the second is in the nature of a hybrid, partaking of the features of both par value and no-par value stock.

LEGAL
CAPITAL

Since there is generally no liability of the stockholders of a corporation for its debts the state laws, in order to protect the creditors, place a restriction on the amount of assets, measured in terms of money, that a corporation may distribute to its stockholders. That restriction is represented by the *legal* or *stated capital*.

Just what constitutes the legal capital of a certain corporation may be determined by referring to the state statute under which the corporation is organized. However, the following generalizations may

202

be made: (1) if the stock has a par value the legal capital is the total par value of all stock issued; (2) if the stock is without par value but has a stated value per share the legal capital is the total stated value of the stock issued, plus such amounts as the board of directors may add thereto; (3) if the stock is without par value or stated value and there are no special provisions in the law, the legal capital is the total consideration received from the stockholders for the stock.

It is important that the accountant indicate the legal capital in the accounts and in the balance sheet of the corporation.

SURPLUS (RETAINED EARNINGS)

It has been shown how the balance of the Profit and Loss account of an individual proprietorship is closed into the Capital account. Similar procedure is followed in accounting for a partnership.

The balance of the Profit and Loss account of a corporation, however, is not closed into the Capital Stock account or accounts. The reason is that these accounts are required to indicate the legal capital that must be retained in the business for the protection of creditors. The net income or net loss is, therefore, carried to a separate account called Surplus, or Retained Earnings. The credit balance of this account indicates the maximum amount that may be distributed to the stockholders as dividends.

If the Surplus account has a debit balance, as a result of losses sustained, such balance is referred to as a *deficit*. The amount of the deficit is the measure of the impairment of the capital. Under such conditions the name of the account is automatically changed to Deficit.

CAPITAL SURPLUS

A surplus, or addition to capital, may arise in other ways than through earnings. An illustration is afforded by the case of a corporation that receives land on which to erect a plant as a gift from a municipality desiring to attract business. Such addition to capital is not credited to the Surplus (Retained Earnings) account to which the net income is carried but to a separate account with the title Capital Surplus.

For example, if a certain corporation is given land the reasonable market price of which is $10,000.00, the entry is:

```
Land .................................................................. 10,000.00
    Capital surplus ....................................                 10,000.00
        To record gift of land by city.
```

Since there are reasons for additions to capital other than earnings

203

and gifts, as will be shown presently, many accountants have discontinued the use of a single Capital Surplus account and use separate accounts for each of the different types of capital additions. The account used to record the increase in capital through gift might be called Additions to Capital by Gift.

ISSUANCE OF ONE CLASS OF CAPITAL STOCK

When capital stock is issued by a corporation having but one class of capital stock, the accounting entry consists of a debit to the account for the asset received and a credit to Capital Stock.

Let us assume that a certain corporation having only one class of stock with a par value of $100.00 receives from J. Smith, an investor, $1,000.00 in payment for 10 shares. The entry is:

```
Cash ................................................................ 1,000.00
    Capital stock ........................................             1,000.00
    Issue of 10 shares to J. Smith.
```

The same accounts would be debited and credited if the stock had no par value. For example, if a corporation issues 500 shares of capital stock without par value to T. Jones at $10.00 a share the entry is:

```
Cash ................................................................ 5,000.00
    Capital stock ........................................             5,000.00
    Issue of 500 shares to T. Jones.
```

The consideration, however, may not necessarily be in the form of cash. For example, if 1,000 shares of capital stock with a par value of $100.00 are issued to R. Green for a building, the entry is:

```
Building ........................................................100,000.00
    Capital stock ........................................         100,000.00
    Issue of 1,000 shares to R. Green.
```

Capital stock may also be issued for services rendered to the corporation. Stock is often issued for legal or other services performed at the time the corporation is organized. In such event the debit is to the account Organization Expense. Thus the entry for the issue of 20 shares of capital stock with a par value of $100.00 to H. Frey for organization services is: .

```
Organization expense ....................................... 2,000.00
    Capital stock ........................................             2,000.00
    Issue of 20 shares to H. Frey.
```

ORGANIZATION EXPENSE

It is not reasonable to deduct organization expense from the income of the first year of operation. In fact, this cost is logically applicable to all the years of the existence of the corporation. However, the organization expense is amortized as a deduction from the income of a reasonable number of years, usually from three to five, depending on the amount of the expense.

During the years over which the organization expense is amortized, the unamortized portion is an asset of the corporation and is classified as a *deferred charge*. Deferred charges are similar to prepaid expenses. The distinction between deferred charges and prepaid expenses is that the deferred charges are types of expense that do not occur commonly, while the prepaid expenses are types that are constantly incurred in connection with the routine operation of the business, such as insurance and office supplies.

As has been shown, the prepaid expenses are classified as current assets. The deferred charges are placed in a separate category and listed in the balance sheet after the fixed assets. Some accountants, however, place the prepaid expenses in the balance sheet with the deferred charges.

If a corporation issues more than one class of stock a separate account is kept with each class. For example, if $2,000.00 of preferred stock is issued to B. Wall for cash and $3,000.00 of common stock is issued to L. Chase for cash, the entries are: **SEVERAL CLASSES OF STOCK**

Cash	2,000.00	
Capital stock—Preferred		2,000.00
Issue of 20 shares to B. Wall.		
Cash	3,000.00	
Capital stock—Common..		3,000.00
Issue of 30 shares to L. Chase.		

Sometimes stock is sold on installment. Since stock is usually not issued until paid for, the account Capital Stock Subscribed is credited and an account with the subscribers, in the nature of an account receivable, is debited. Thus, if $10,000.00 is subscribed the entry is: **SALE OF STOCK ON INSTALLMENT**

Subscribers to capital stock	10,000.00	
Capital stock subscribed		10,000.00
To record subscription.		

The account with the subscribers is credited for all installments paid. Thus, if $1,000.00 is paid the entry is:

205

Cash 1,000.00
    Subscribers to capital stock 1,000.00
    To record installment payment.

When all installments have been paid the stock is issued and the following entry is made:

Capital stock subscribed 10,000.00
    Capital stock 10,000.00
    To record issue of capital stock.

In order to provide a record of the payment of all subscriptions, the above procedure may be followed even though the stock is not sold on installment. This is particularly desirable if there are many subscribers.

NO-PAR VALUE STOCK WITH STATED VALUE

The entry for the issue of no-par value stock without a stated value is exactly like that for the issue of par value stock. But in the case of no-par value stock with a stated value the entry will depend on the requirements of the laws of the state in which the corporation is incorporated. Some states require that the entire consideration received for the stock be credited to the Capital Stock account while others permit the crediting of only the stated value to the Capital Stock account and any amount above the stated value to a Capital Surplus account. Some accountants call the account used for this purpose Paid-In Surplus, while others give it such title as Capital in Excess of Stated Value.

To illustrate, let it be assumed that a certain corporation authorized to issue no-par value stock with a stated value of $10.00 per share sells 100 shares at $15.00 a share. If the corporation is incorporated under the laws of a state which requires that the entire consideration be credited to the Capital Stock account the entry is:

Cash 1,500.00
    Capital stock 1,500.00
    To record issue of 100 shares.

But if the corporation is incorporated under the laws of a state that permits the amount above the stated value to be credited to a Surplus account the entry may be as above or:

Cash 1,500.00
    Capital stock 1,000.00
    Paid-in surplus 500.00
    To record issue of 100 shares.

206

However, at the discretion of the board of directors, any part of the $500.00 in excess of stated value might be credited to Capital Stock and the remainder to Paid-In Surplus.

Capital stock with a par value may be sold by the corporation for an amount above the par value. The excess above the par value constitutes a *premium* and this is credited to the Capital Surplus account, or an account with such title as Capital in Excess of Par.

PREMIUM ON CAPITAL STOCK

For example, let it be assumed that a certain corporation sells 10 shares of its capital stock having a par of $100.00 for $105.00 a share. The entry is:

```
Cash ............................................................... 1,050.00
    Capital stock.....................................................     1,000.00
    Capital surplus .................................................        50.00
    To record sale of 10 shares.
```

The laws of only a few states permit the issue of stock at a *discount*. Under the laws of the other states, stock with a par value sold below par is regarded as stock not fully paid for and the purchaser thereof is liable for the balance due on his stock subscription.

DISCOUNT ON CAPITAL STOCK

Both in states that recognize a discount on capital stock and those that do not, the purchaser of par value stock sold below par may be forced by creditors of the corporation to pay in the difference between the par value of the stock and the amount paid for it in case the corporation is unable to pay its debts. As a result of this contingent liability it is not likely that investors will want to own such stock. Consequently, there is very little stock sold at a discount in existence. This is also so because a corporation unable to sell stock with a par value at par will obviously elect to issue no-par value stock.

The entry for stock sold at a discount is similar to that for stock sold at a premium except that instead of a credit for the premium there is a debit for the discount. This debit is preferably to an account Discount on Capital Stock. The entry for 10 shares of $100.00 par value stock sold for $95.00 a share is:

```
Cash ............................................................... 950.00
Discount on capital stock ............................................  50.00
    Capital stock.....................................................     1,000.00
    To record sale of 10 shares.
```

There is a difference of opinion among accountants whether the

207

discount may be debited to any existing surplus; also whether it may be offset against the premium on other stock issued by the corporation. The discussion is rather academic since the issue is rarely, if ever, raised in practice.

TREASURY STOCK

Stock fully paid for and issued and later reacquired by the corporation is known as *treasury stock,* also called *reacquired shares.* It may be reacquired either through purchase by the corporation or through donation by stockholders.

Treasury stock should not be confused with unissued stock which is sometimes erroneously referred to as "treasury stock."

There are various reasons for the creation of treasury stock. A corporation may purchase its own stock in order to create a market demand and as a result raise the market price. Stockholders may donate stock to the corporation in order to enable it to obtain funds that cannot be obtained in other ways. A corporation unable to sell its unissued stock at par may sell treasury stock below par without a contingent liability to the purchaser since the stock was sold at par when originally issued.

Purchases by a corporation of its own outstanding stock are limited by law to the extent of its surplus available for dividends. This limitation has been written into the laws in order that the legal or stated capital of the corporation will not be reduced. The principle involved is that the amount of net assets represented by the legal capital may not be dissipated by the corporation but must be held intact in order to protect the creditors, as we have already seen. When stock has been purchased for the creation of treasury stock the surplus available for dividends is *restricted* to the extent of the sum paid for the stock, that is, the remaining surplus after deducting the amount paid for the stock measures the extent to which surplus is available for dividends.

The commonly accepted entry for the purchase of stock for the treasury is a debit to an account Treasury Stock and a credit to Cash. Thus, the purchase by a corporation of 100 shares of its own $100.00 par value stock at $95.00 a share is recorded as follows:

Treasury stock...	9,500.00	
Cash		9,500.00
To record purchase of 100 shares.		

The entry would be the same if the stock had no par value.

When treasury stock is sold above or below the purchase price a profit or loss results. If, for instance, the above treasury stock is sold at $97.00 a share, the entry is:

Cash	9,700.00	
Treasury stock		9,500.00
Profit on sale of treasury stock		200.00
To record sale of 100 shares.		

The profit on the sale will be closed into Profit and Loss at the end of the period.

If, however, the treasury stock had been held for a considerable period of time and there was clearly no intention of profit-making involved, the $200.00 excess of the sale price over the purchase price might be credited to Capital Surplus, or one of its subdivisions with appropriate title.

When stock is donated to the corporation by stockholders the preferable procedure is not to make an entry in the books of account until the stock is sold. At this time the entry consists of a debit to Cash and a credit to Capital Surplus or to an account with such title as Addition to Capital by Donation. Thus, the entry for the sale of 100 shares of $100.00 par value donated stock sold at $95.00 per share is:

Cash	9,500.00	
Capital surplus		9,500.00
To record sale of 100 shares donated stock.		

CAPITAL OF A CORPORATION From the foregoing it is evident that the capital of a corporation is the total of the balance of the Capital Stock account, or accounts, plus the balances of all forms of Surplus accounts.

STOCK VALUES A share of stock may have a *par value,* as was shown above. It may have a *market value:* the price at which it may be purchased in the stock market. It also has what is known as a *book value* which consists of the legal capital represented by each share, plus any surplus belonging thereto since an aliquot part of the surplus belongs to each share.

BOOK VALUE OF A SHARE OF STOCK The book value of a share of preferred stock is usually the credit balance in the Capital Stock—Preferred account divided by the number of shares outstanding. However, if the preferred stockholders have a claim on the surplus, as in the case of participating preferred stock or cumulative preferred stock with dividends in arrears, the amount of such claim is added before dividing by the number of shares outstanding.

In the absence of any participating preferred stock or any cumulative preferred stock with dividends in arrears, the book value of a share of common stock is obtained by dividing the total of the balances of the Capital Stock—Common account and Surplus accounts by the number of shares outstanding. Appropriate deductions from the Surplus should be made for any claims of the preferred stockholders thereon.

BOOKS PECU-
LIAR TO THE
CORPORATION

The *minute book,* kept by corporations, is not part of the accounting records but the source of important information for the accountant. In it are recorded the charter or articles of incorporation and the actions of the directors and stockholders at their meetings: bylaws, resolutions, and so forth. The accountant refers to this book for data that are the basis of various entries in the books of account.

The *stock certificate book* contains the stock certificate forms. In addition it contains stubs from which the certificates, when filled out with the names of stockholders and the number of shares owned by them, are separated. On the stubs is entered a record of the stockholders and their holdings.

The *stockholders' ledger* is used by corporations having many stockholders since a stock certificate book record would not be adequate. The stockholders' ledger contains an account with each stockholder. In the account an entry is made for each acquisition and each transfer of stock, the balance indicating the number of shares owned. The stockholders' ledger is a subsidiary ledger controlled by the general ledger account Capital Stock.

The *stock transfer book* is a book of original entry used as the basis for postings to the stockholders' ledger. An entry is made for each transfer of stock from one stockholder to another.

32. Corporations: Earnings

THE EARNINGS of a corporation are either distributed to the stock-holders or retained in the business. Distribution to the stockholders is made in the form of dividends. Retention of earnings is reflected in the accounts by carrying the net income to the Surplus or Retained Earnings account.

The payment of dividends rests with the board of directors. No dividend may be paid unless the directors take formal action at a meeting of the board to declare a dividend. But once declared, the dividend becomes a current liability of the corporation and must be paid. The usual procedure is to declare the dividend as payable to the stockholders of record as of a certain date, the dividend actually to be paid at a later date. This allows time for preparing the dividend checks. DIVIDENDS

Although a corporation may have a sufficiently large surplus available, the directors are not obliged to declare a dividend if they do not see fit to do so. Unless it can be shown that their acts are fraudulent, arbitrary, or oppressive the stockholders cannot take legal action to compel them to declare a dividend. It is assumed that the directors act in good faith and in the best interests of the business; and if at any time the stockholders are dissatisfied with the dividend policy of the board they may elect other directors at their next meeting.

A dividend on par value stock is usually declared as a certain percentage of par while a dividend on no-par value stock is declared as a certain sum per share. To illustrate, let it be assumed that the directors of a certain corporation that has outstanding 100,000 shares of no-par value common stock and $50,000.00 of 6 per cent preferred stock, par $100.00, declare a dividend of 10 cents a share on the common stock and the regular dividend on the preferred stock. The entry is:

Surplus	13,000.00	
Dividends payable...		13,000.00

To record declaration of a dividend of 10
cents a share on common stock, $10,000.00,
and the regular 6 per cent dividend on preferred stock, $3,000.00.

When the dividend is paid the entry is:

Dividends payable..	13,000.00	
Cash...		13,000.00

To record payment of dividend.

Although dividends are commonly paid in cash they are sometimes paid in the form of assets other than cash as in the case of a certain distilling corporation which paid a dividend in liquor.

STOCK
DIVIDENDS

A dividend may also be paid in shares of the capital stock of the corporation. For example, if a certain corporation with $1,000,000.00 stock, par $100.00, outstanding declares a 25 per cent stock dividend the entry is:

Surplus	250,000.00	
Stock dividend payable...................................		250,000.00

To record declaration of a 25 per cent stock
dividend.

When the dividend is paid the entry is:

Stock dividend payable..	250,000.00	
Capital stock		250,000.00

To record issue of capital stock as a stock
dividend.

A stock dividend has the effect of converting retained earnings into permanent capital and does not change a stockholder's equity in the corporation. If in the above case we assume that before the stock dividend the Surplus amounted to $500,000.00, the capital then was $1,500,000.00 and the equity per share $150.00.

After the stock dividend the Capital Stock account shows a balance of $1,250,000.00, representing 12,500 shares with a Surplus of $250,000.00, leaving the capital the same $1,500,000.00. But since there are now outstanding 12,500 shares, the equity per share is $120.00.

To show that the stock dividend did not affect a stockholder's equity, let us take the case of a stockholder who owned four shares

212

before the stock dividend. His equity was 4 × $150.00, or $600.00. After the stock dividend he owned five shares but his equity remained the same, 5 × $120.00, or $600.00.

A portion of the retained earnings may be appropriated for a specific purpose and thus made unavailable for disbursement to stockholders as dividends. The restriction of the dividends may be merely at the discretion of the board of directors or it may have a legal basis.

A restriction of the amount available for dividend purposes may be made, for example, when the corporation is planning an extension of plant facilities and consequently the board of directors chooses to retain a sufficiently large portion of the corporation's wealth within the business for this purpose. The entry to create such a reserve amounting to $10,000.00 is:

SURPLUS RESERVES

```
Surplus ...................................................................... 10,000.00
    Reserve for plant extension................................    10,000.00
        To create a reserve for plant extension.
```

When the plant extension has been completed and paid for, the restriction of dividends is no longer necessary and the amount of the reserve is *restored to Surplus* by the entry:

```
Reserve for plant extension........................................ 10,000.00
    Surplus ..................................................................    10,000.00
        To restore reserve to Surplus.
```

Sometimes a reserve representing a subdivision of surplus is created because of a legal restriction on the surplus. This occurs when the corporation has borrowed money and has made an agreement with the lenders that a certain portion of its surplus shall not be available for dividends, or when a restriction has been placed on the surplus by the courts as a result of litigation.

Surplus reserves are sometimes referred to as *appropriated surplus,* the remaining surplus being called *free surplus*.

Surplus reserves are shown in the balance sheet immediately after the free surplus and are added thereto since they are part of the surplus.

33. Corporations: Anticipated Costs and Losses

IT IS A PRINCIPLE of accounting that the accountant should provide, by a deduction from income, for all foreseeable costs and losses that can reasonably be assigned to the period under review. While well established in certain areas, in others the application of this principle is vague.

PROVISION FOR
BAD DEBTS

The most common application of the principle under discussion is that of the provision for bad debts. Here, as has been seen, on the basis of the experience of the business, the accountant makes a deduction from income for the anticipated loss on the receivables as of the last day of the accounting period, the corresponding credit being to the Allowance for Bad Debts. The loss, of course, has not occurred but it is assigned to the period under review because the sales from which the receivables arose took place in that period. It is quite logical to make the deduction for the loss on bad debts from the income of the period since the bad debts represent the portion of the stated income that will not be collected. The deduction thus reduces the income to the amount that it is believed will be realized. When the losses actually occur in the ensuing period they are debited to the Allowance for Bad Debts, thus offsetting the allowance made in advance.

PROVISION FOR
WARRANTY

The provision for bad debts is for an anticipated loss. Let us now review a provision for an anticipated cost.

In cases where a warranty has been given on the product sold, a deduction from the sales income should be made in anticipation of the cost of meeting claims as a result of the warranty. This is, of course, fitting and proper since the sales income that will be realized is the amount of the invoiced prices of the sales less the cost of maintaining the warranty. The deduction from income is made on the basis of an estimate and is credited to an appropriate account to show the estimated liability. When payments are made on warranty claims this ac-

214

count is debited, the payments thus offsetting the credit for the pro-vision made in advance. The accounts for estimated liabilities are commonly called *liability reserves*.

If it should be found that the warranty claims have over a period of years been overestimated, the excess is *restored to income,* that is, it is treated as a special credit to income.

Another loss often provided for in anticipation is loss by fire. The **PROVISION FOR** liability account credited is usually called the Reserve for Self- **FIRE LOSSES** Insurance, although this is really a misnomer since no self-insurance takes place; that is, there is usually no fund created to compensate for the loss in case of fire. What is done is merely to make a deduc-tion from income in anticipation of the loss. When a loss occurs its amount is debited to the reserve account.

In this case the allocation to the period may be questioned. Bad debts losses and warranty costs may readily be assigned to the pe-riod in which the sales to which they apply were made. But can it be held that losses by fire can be assigned to periods other than those in which they occur? In spite of this, it has become customary in certain lines of business where fires are likely to occur as, for example, in a large chain of stores, to make provision in advance for loss by fire. The principle of provision for losses in anticipation has thus been expanded to a type of loss that cannot readily be assigned to a period in advance of that in which the loss occurs. This procedure may, how-ever, be justified on the basis of conservatism.

In similar manner other types of losses are provided for. Among **OTHER LOSSES** them one finds such losses as those of loss of cash in closed bank, **AND COSTS** loss on investments, loss of property in a theater of war or in enemy **PROVIDED FOR** territory, loss by flood, and loss by pilferage. Anticipated costs such as pensions and property maintenance and replacement are provided for.

While all the reserves for anticipated costs and losses are of the **POSITION OF** same nature some are shown in the balance sheet as deductions from **RESERVES IN** related assets while others are listed as liabilities. The Allowance **BALANCE** for Bad Debts is deducted from the Accounts and Notes Receivable to **SHEET** which it applies; a Reserve for Cash in Closed Bank is deducted from Cash in Closed Bank; a Reserve for Loss on Investments is deducted from the item Investments; a Reserve for Loss of Property in Theater of War is deducted from the asset to which it relates.

On the other hand, the reserves for costs and losses that do not relate to specific assets are shown among the liabilities, commonly in a section headed *Reserves*. Among these are such as Reserve for Warranty, Reserve for Self-Insurance, Reserve for Flood Losses, Reserve for Repainting Stores, and so forth.

Some accountants refer to allowances or reserves deducted from assets as *valuation reserves* and those shown among the liabilities as *liability reserves*. However, because the reserves for anticipated costs and losses are all of the same nature it might be well to give the same designation to all. They might properly be called *income reserves* since they are created by deductions from current income, in contrast to the reserves that are created by appropriations of retained earnings discussed in Chapter 32.

34. Corporations: Bonds

THE LONG-TERM DEBT of a corporation is usually created by borrowing. And because it is usually not possible for the corporation to obtain a large enough loan from one source, the total of the loan is divided into parts, commonly of $1,000.00 each, and each part is represented by an instrument known as a *bond*.

Those who buy and thus invest in bonds are known as *bondholders*. They are creditors of the corporation, in contrast to the stockholders who are the owners.

A bond is in the nature of a promise to pay a specified sum of money at a certain time; it is thus similar to a promissory note. The important distinction, however, is the element of time: promissory notes are usually for short periods such as thirty, sixty, or ninety days, whereas bonds run for five, ten, twenty, and even more years. Bonds are more elaborate in form than notes and bear the corporate seal.

Bonds bear interest; and because of the length of time they have to run the interest is not all paid at maturity, as in the case of a note, but periodically, commonly semiannually.

The process of combining various debts into one large debt or fund is known as *funding* the debt. And because the corporation frequently uses the money obtained through an issue of bonds to pay off various debts, the bonds of a corporation are commonly referred to as its *funded debt*.

A bond, like a note, may be secured or unsecured. If secured, the security is commonly in the form of a mortgage either on real property or on equipment. Bonds so secured are known as *mortgage bonds*. And since there may be more than one mortgage, the bonds are named First Mortgage Bonds, Second Mortgage Bonds, etc. Unsecured bonds are based on the general credit standing of the corporation and are known as *debenture bonds*.

The mortgage securing a bond issue is given to a trustee who acts in behalf of the bondholders. The function of trustee is usually performed by a bank or trust company. A document known as a *trust indenture* is prepared and signed by both the trustee and the corporation. The indenture states the terms of the bond issue: par value of the bonds, total to be issued, interest rate, maturity date, and other pertinent facts.

Bonds may be *registered bonds,* in which case the names and addresses of the bondholders are registered with the corporation and at each interest date checks for the interest are sent to the bondholders. However, the bonds may be of the type known as *coupon bonds.* If so, the bondholders are not registered with the corporation and collect their periodic interest by means of coupons attached to the bonds, one for each interest payment, which are clipped and cashed or deposited in a bank like a check.

MARKETING
OF BONDS

Corporate bonds are most commonly disposed of through an investment banking house, or group of such houses known as a *syndicate,* who "underwrite" the issue, that is, they agree to buy the issue from the corporation at a certain price. The underwriters sell the bonds to their clients, usually at a higher price. Some bonds, however, are disposed of by "direct sale," in which case one purchaser, such as an insurance company, might buy the entire issue.

Upon disposing of an issue of bonds the corporation may receive the par amount, or it may receive more or less than the par. When the corporation receives less than the par for the bonds, they are said to have been sold at a *discount;* and when the corporation receives more than the par, the bonds are said to have been sold at a *premium.*

The discount or premium is usually a composite of several items. It may comprise, for example, a precise adjustment of the stated interest rate and also an element of expense such as the fee of the investment bankers who underwrite the issue. Because of differences in market conditions and marketing methods, industrial bonds are commonly disposed of at a discount and public utility bonds at a premium.

Although bonds are usually issued in $1,000.00 denominations, they are quoted for convenience as though they were in $100.00 denominations. A $1,000.00 bond to be sold for $1,050.00 is quoted at 105; and if to be sold at $950.00 is quoted at 95.

METHODS OF
REDEMPTION

Since the redemption of a bond issue by the corporation at one time out of current funds is usually not convenient, various schemes are used to facilitate the retirement process. One method is to issue the bonds in several "series," each series being redeemable at a certain date. Such bonds are known as *serial bonds.*

A second method is to retire a certain number of bonds, usually at the option of the corporation, at any interest date. Such bonds are known as *callable bonds*. It is usually agreed that a premium will be paid to the bondholder when the bonds are called.

A third method is to issue *sinking fund bonds*. Under this method periodic payments of an agreed sum are made by the corporation to the trustee. The trustee may either accumulate the sums paid in a *sinking fund* until the date of maturity of the bond issue, investing the money to earn interest which is added to the fund; or he may call bonds for redemption periodically, thus gradually reducing the corporation's funded debt. The latter plan is favored at the present time.

The entry for the sale at par of a $500,000.00 issue of 10-year, 6 per cent, First Mortgage Bonds, due January 1, 1966, is:

```
Cash ........................................................................ 500,000.00
        10-year, 6%, First Mortgage Bonds,
                  due January 1, 1966 ..................         500,000.00
        Sale of bonds at par.
```

If the bonds are sold for $475,000.00, that is, at a discount of $25,000.00, the entry is:

```
Cash ........................................................................ 475,000.00
Bond discount ........................................................  25,000.00
        10-year, 6%, First Mortgage Bonds,
                  due January 1, 1966 ..................         500,000.00
        Sale of bonds at 95.
```

The account Bond Discount is treated as a deferred charge and is amortized over the life of the bond issue. In the above case, since the bonds are to run for ten years, the amortization of the discount is $2,500.00 per year. At the end of each year the entry for the amortization is:

```
Amortization of bond discount............................... 2,500.00
        Bond discount ...............................................         2,500.00
        To amortize bond discount for one year.
```

Assuming that the interest on the above bonds is payable semi-annually, the entry for the interest payment on July 1, 1956, is:

```
Bond interest expense ............................................ 15,000.00
        Cash ................................................................         15,000.00
        Payment of semiannual bond interest.
```

If the bonds are sold for $525,000.00, that is, at a premium of $25,000.00, the entry is:

Cash 525,000.00
    10-year, 6%, First Mortgage Bonds,
            due January 1, 1966 ....   500,000.00
      Bond premium...   25,000.00
  Sale of bonds at 105.

The bond premium is treated as a deferred credit. This is placed in the same category as deferred income.

The entry for the amortization of the bond premium for each year is:

Bond premium... 2,500.00
    Amortization of bond premium 2,500.00
  To amortize bond premium for one year.

The amortization creates an addition to income since the bond premium is income applying to ten years that was received in advance.

The entry for the redemption of the bonds at maturity is:

10-year, 6%, First Mortgage Bonds,
         due January 1, 1966 .... 500,000.00
    Cash 500,000.00
  Redemption of bonds.

A similar entry is made when part of an issue is called for redemption. Although the cash would be paid to the trustee before the bonds are actually redeemed, the account with the bonds payable is usually debited at the time of the payment to the trustee, it being assumed that the corporation has settled its liability to the bondholders since the trustee represents them.

35. Corporations: Financial Statements

THE BALANCE SHEET of the Mantuco Corporation as of December 31, 1956, shown on page 222, will serve to illustrate some of the features of the corporate balance sheet.

It should be noted that for each class of stock it is stated whether the stock has a par value or not; and if it has a par value or a stated value, this is indicated. This description is followed by a statement of the number of shares authorized and issued. The amount credited in the account for the stock issued is then extended.

As stated in Chapter 31, the preferred treatment of treasury stock is to carry it at cost. It is then shown as a deduction from the total capital stock and surplus. Information regarding the restriction on surplus with respect to dividends because of the purchase of stock for the treasury is shown parenthetically.

The reserves for anticipated costs and losses are listed in a section at the end of the liabilities and preceding the capital stock.

It is common practice for corporations to invest cash not currently needed in readily marketable securities, usually government bonds, until such time as the cash is required. Such temporary investments are listed in the balance sheet immediately after the cash and are usually carried at cost. If there is an appreciable difference between cost and market, the market price is indicated parenthetically.

The nominal amount of $1.00 for goodwill indicates that at some time in the past a payment was made for goodwill, probably upon the acquisition of a business, but that this has been written down by a debit to Surplus, the $1.00 being retained merely to indicate that the business possesses excess earning power. Such procedure has in recent times become common because of a recognition of the fact that the item *goodwill* does not present any usable measure of the excess earning power.

The income statement of the Mantuco Corporation for the year ended December 31, 1956, is shown on page 223 in somewhat condensed form since the details of the cost of goods sold and the selling, general, and administrative expenses are not given.

THE BALANCE SHEET

THE INCOME STATEMENT

MANTUCO CORPORATION
BALANCE SHEET
DECEMBER 31, 1956

Assets

CURRENT ASSETS:

Cash		$ 37,296.85	
Marketable securities, at cost (market $24,670.00)		25,580.00	
Accounts receivable	$ 178,297.25		
Less Estimated bad debts	3,250.00	175,047.25	
Inventory (at the lower of cost or market)		639,258.63	
Prepaid expenses		12,165.80	
Total current assets			$ 889,348.53

PROPERTY, PLANT, AND EQUIPMENT:

Land and building	$1,854,056.93		
Less Depreciation	387,958.72	$1,466,098.21	
Equipment	$ 343,753.52		
Less Depreciation	98,201.64	245,551.88	
Total property, plant, and equipment			1,711,650.09

GOODWILL	1.00

DEFERRED CHARGES:

Bond discount	4,800.00

OTHER ASSETS:

Accounts receivable (not current)	$ 5,000.00	
Miscellaneous advances and deposits	7,500.00	
Total other assets		12,500.00

	$2,618,299.62

Liabilities and Capital

CURRENT LIABILITIES:

Accounts payable	$ 144,297.54	
Accrued expenses	17,436.02	
Dividends payable	102,500.00	
Federal income tax payable	137,584.29	
Total current liabilities		$ 401,817.85

FUNDED DEBT:

First mortgage, 5-year, 6% bonds, due January 1, 1960	100,000.00

RESERVES:

Reserve for warranty	$ 47,285.20	
Reserve for fire loss	21,750.00	
Total reserves		69,035.20

CAPITAL STOCK:

7% cumulative preferred stock, par $100.00		
Authorized and issued, 2,000 shares	$ 200,000.00	
Common stock, no par, stated value $5.00		
Authorized, 500,000 shares		
Issued, 300,000 shares	1,500,000.00	
Total capital stock		$1,700,000.00

EARNED SURPLUS (restricted $30,000.00 because of purchase of stock for the treasury)

	77,446.57

PAID-IN SURPLUS

	300,000.00
	$2,077,446.57

Less Treasury stock—Common		
5,000 shares, at cost	30,000.00	
Total capital		2,047,446.57

	$2,618,299.62

MANTUCO CORPORATION
INCOME STATEMENT
FOR THE YEAR ENDED DECEMBER 31, 1956

Gross sales, less discounts, returns, and allowances		$2,352,791.27
Cost of goods sold		953,228.34
Gross profit		$1,399,562.93

EXPENSES:

Selling, general, and administrative expenses	$895,621.96	
Provision for depreciation	182,697.25	
Provision for bad debts	2,750.00	
Total expenses		1,081,069.21
		$ 318,493.72

CHARGES TO INCOME:

Provision for warranty	$ 20,500.00	
Provision for fire loss	8,350.00	
Interest expense	6,782.54	
Amortization of bond discount	1,600.00	
Total charges to income		37,232.54
		$ 281,261.18

OTHER INCOME:

Profit on sale of securities	$ 1,497.52	
Interest on investments	2,654.20	
Profit on sale of equipment	1,875.00	
Total other income		6,026.72
Net income before federal income tax		$ 287,287.90
Federal income tax		143,840.27
Net income for the year		$ 143,447.63

MANTUCO CORPORATION
EARNED SURPLUS STATEMENT
FOR THE YEAR ENDED DECEMBER 31, 1956

Earned surplus, January 1		$ 35,773.94
Add Net income for the year		143,447.63
Adjustment of 1955 depreciation		725.00
		$ 179,946.57
Less Dividend on 7% preferred stock	$ 14,000.00	
Dividend on common stock, $.30 per share	88,500.00	102,500.00
Earned surplus, December 31		$ 77,446.57

There is little difference between the corporate income statement and that of the other forms of ownership organization. It is worthy of note, however, how the provisions for anticipated costs and losses and the federal income tax are shown.

In recent times the scope of the income statement has been expanded considerably. It formerly was held that the income statement should comprise only those matters that affect the net income derived from the regular operations of the business and that the other forms of income and expense should not appear in the statement and should be closed into Surplus instead of into Profit and Loss. The contemporary attitude toward the matter, however, is that all manner of income and expense should be included in the statement, whether regular or extraordinary, since all gains and losses affect the position of the business and are of interest to the reader of the statement.

As a result of the procedure of carrying all gains and losses to the Profit and Loss account and showing them in the income statement, very few entries are made directly to the Surplus account. This procedure has been called the *clean surplus* procedure.

THE EARNED
SURPLUS
STATEMENT

It is now customary for corporations to include with their financial statements an earned surplus statement which shows the earned surplus at the beginning of the period, the additions thereto, the deductions therefrom, and the earned surplus at the end of the period. The earned surplus statement of the Mantuco Corporation for the year ended December 31, 1956, is on page 223.

Some corporations combine the income statement and the earned surplus statement into one statement. This is effected by tabulating the income statement and adding to the net income the earned surplus at the beginning of the period and any additions thereto, and subtracting the deductions therefrom to arrive at the earned surplus at the end of the period.

THE POSITION
STATEMENT

There has in recent years come into use a form for the balance sheet usually referred to as the "position statement" form, although, as was stated in Chapter 16, any balance sheet might be called a position statement. Such a form of balance sheet for the Mantuco Corporation is shown on page 225. In this statement alternative terminology to that in the balance sheet on page 222 has been used in order to acquaint the reader with such alternative and newer terminology.

224

MANTUCO CORPORATION
POSITION STATEMENT
DECEMBER 31, 1956

CURRENT ASSETS:

Cash		$ 37,296.85	
Marketable securities, at cost (market $24,670.00)		25,580.00	
Accounts receivable	$ 178,297.25		
Less Estimated bad debts	3,250.00	175,047.25	
Inventory (at the lower of cost or market)		639,258.63	
Prepaid expenses		12,165.80	
Total current assets			$ 889,348.53

CURRENT LIABILITIES:

Accounts payable		$ 144,297.54	
Accrued expenses		17,436.02	
Dividends payable		102,500.00	
Federal income tax payable		137,584.29	
Total current liabilities			401,817.85
Working capital			$ 487,530.68

PROPERTY, PLANT, AND EQUIPMENT:

Land and building	$1,854,056.93		
Less Depreciation	387,958.72	$1,466,098.21	
Equipment	$ 343,753.52		
Less Depreciation	98,201.64	245,551.88	
Total property, plant, and equipment			1,711,650.09

GOODWILL 1.00

DEFERRED CHARGES:

Bond discount 4,800.00

OTHER ASSETS:

Accounts receivable (not current)	$ 5,000.00	
Miscellaneous advances and deposits	7,500.00	
Total other assets		12,500.00
Total assets, less current liabilities		$2,216,481.77

FUNDED DEBT:

First mortgage, 5-year, 6% bonds, due January 1, 1960		100,000.00
		$2,116,481.77

RESERVES:

Reserve for warranty	$ 47,285.20	
Reserve for fire loss	21,750.00	
Total reserves		69,035.20
Excess of assets over liabilities (stockholders' equity)		$2,047,446.57

REPRESENTED BY:

7% cumulative preferred stock, par $100.00	
Authorized and issued, 2,000 shares	$ 200,000.00
Common stock, no par, stated value $5.00	
Authorized, 500,000 shares	
Issued, 300,000 shares	1,500,000.00
Total capital stock	$1,700,000.00
Retained earnings (restricted $30,000.00 because of purchase of stock for the treasury)	77,446.57
Capital in excess of stated value of common stock	300,000.00
	$2,077,446.57
Less Treasury stock—Common	
5,000 shares, at cost	30,000.00
	$2,047,446.57

THE SINGLE-
STEP INCOME
STATEMENT

A form of income statement commonly employed by corporations in their annual reports to stockholders is the "single-step" form, in contrast with the traditional form now referred to as the "multiple-step" form. In the single-step form all kinds of income are grouped together and from the total, the total of the expenses, also grouped together, is deducted, in a single operation or step, to arrive at the net income for the year. Such a statement, combined with that of earned surplus or retained earnings, for the Mantuco Corporation is illustrated on page 227.

CONSOLIDATED
STATEMENTS

When a corporation owns all of, or a controlling interest in, the stock of another corporation, the owning corporation is known as the *parent company* and the owned corporation as a *subsidiary company*. Such ownership of one corporation, evidenced by ownership of capital stock, is a common practice in the organization of modern business.

The parent company and each of its subsidiaries are legally independent entities. Each has its own accounting records and prepares its own financial statements. However, from a realistic point of view the parent and its subsidiaries constitute one organization. It is, therefore, more informative to those interested in the organization to have statements that show the income and the financial position of the organization as a whole. Such financial statements are usually prepared by accountants; they are called *consolidated statements*.

The process of consolidating the statements of the parent company and its subsidiaries into one set of statements constitutes an advanced phase of accounting technique beyond the scope of this book. It includes such matters as the elimination of intercompany transactions—for example, the purchase of goods by one of the related companies from another. A transaction of this nature is reflected in an account payable in the books of the purchasing company and an account receivable in the books of the selling company. These items must be eliminated since from the point of view of the organization as a whole such transactions correspond to transactions between departments of a single company.

When a subsidiary company is not wholly owned by the parent company, part of the subsidiary's stock must be owned by others looked upon by the parent company as "outsiders." It is then said that the parent company's interest is the *majority interest,* because it owns the majority of the shares of capital stock, and that the interest of the others is the *minority interest*. Since the consolidated balance sheet

226

MANTUCO CORPORATION
COMBINED INCOME AND RETAINED EARNINGS STATEMENT
FOR THE YEAR ENDED DECEMBER 31, 1956

REVENUE:

Gross sales, less discounts, returns, and allowances	$2,352,791.27
Profit on sale of securities	1,497.52
Interest on investments	2,654.20
Profit on sale of equipment	1,875.00
	$2,358,817.99

DEDUCTIONS FROM REVENUE:

Cost of goods sold	$ 953,228.34
Selling, general, and administrative expenses	895,621.96
Provision for depreciation	182,697.25
Provision for bad debts	2,750.00
Provision for warranty	20,500.00
Provision for fire loss	8,350.00
Interest expense	6,782.54
Amortization of bond discount	1,600.00
Federal income tax	143,840.27
	$2,215,370.36
Net income for the year	$ 143,447.63
Add Retained earnings, January 1	35,773.94
Adjustment of 1955 depreciation	725.00
	$ 179,946.57
Less Dividend on 7% preferred stock................... $14,000.00	
Dividend on common stock, $.30 per share 88,500.00	102,500.00
Retained earnings, December 31	$ 77,446.57

is regarded as that of the majority interest, the minority interest is shown therein as a liability.

Consolidated statements differ very little from the statements of a single corporation. The reader of a statement is, therefore, hardly concerned with the fact that it is a consolidated statement.

INDEX

Index

This book has been composed on the Vari-Typer. The text is in 12 point Garamond No. 620, leaded 1 point. Inserts are in 10 and 8 point Garamond. Financial statement captions are in 10, 7, and 5 point Copperplate Gothic No. 800. All lines have been drawn on the Vari-Typer with Forms Design Segment No. I. The size of the type page is 28½ by 46½ picas.